FIVE STEPS TO BECOME RICH PERSON

AUTHOR: SATYAJEET PATIL.

ABOUT AUTHOR

"Satyajeet Patil has been working with writing challenged clients for over two years. He provides stock market predictions, hacks about getting rich, early retirement plans, investment strategies for students and adults. His educational background in engineering has given her a broad base from which to approach many topics, like algorithm, compounding interests. His writing skills may be confirmed independently on social medias. HE especially enjoys preparing resumes for individuals who are interested in getting rich in early age and who wants investing in stock exchange. You may learn more about his strategies in his Writing as well as in books"

CHAPTER NO 1: INVESTING

Put money in the stock market.

A.   Getting Acquainted with Different Investment Vehicles

B.   Mastering Investment Basics

C.   Starting out

D.   Making the Most of Your Money

Save money for retirement.

A.   Accelerate Retirement Savings According to Your Age

B.   Consider Income-only versus Income & Growth Options

C.   Tips

D.   Warnings

E.   Inflation Warning

Invest in real estate.

A.   Investing Without a Down Payment

B.   Co-Investing for a Down Payment

C.   Borrowing Money for a Down Payment

D.   Finding Properties to Purchase

Invest your time

Avoid purchases that are likely to depreciate rapidly

Choose the right location

A.   Exploring Your Options

B.   Evaluating Aesthetics

C.   Getting Practical

Get entry-level Get entry level job and workup job and work up

A.   Planning Goals for the Future

B.   Making Yourself Invaluable

C.   Broadening Your Skill Set

D.   Advancing Your Career

Change jobs and employers

A.   Starting the Transition

B.   Pounding the Pavement

C.   Finalizing the Transition

CHAPTER NO 3: REDUCING LIVING EXPENSES

TRY EXTREME COUPONING.

A.   . Finding Coupons

B.   Learning to Love Catalina's (In-Store Coupons Generated at the Cash Register)

C.   You Have Coupons, Now Use Them

D.   Other Money Saving Practices

Buy in bulk

A.   What it means to buy in Bulk

B.   Only buy what you need.

C.   Choose items with a long shelf life.

D.   Buy items you're familiar with.

E.   Choose items that are on sale.

F.   When you have a small household.

G.   When you lack storage space.

H.   Before you move or travel.

I.   If you're forced to use your credit card.

J.   Use coupons.

K.   Share with your friends.

L.   Don't forgo quality for a cheap price.

Get a home energy audit

A.   Locate Air Leaks

B.   Seal Air Leaks

C.   Consider Ventilation

D.   Check Insulation

CHAPTER NO 4: Saving Money

Pay yourself first.

Make a budget (and stick to it)

Downgrade your car and house

Cut expenses

CHAPTER NO 1: INVESTING

Put money in the stock market.

Invest money in stocks, bonds, or other vehicles of investment that will give you an annual return on investment (ROI) great enough to sustain you in your retirement. For instance, if you have one million dollars invested and you get a reliable 7% ROI, that's $70,000 per year, less inflation.

Don't get enticed by day traders who tell you it's easy to make a quick buck. Buying and selling dozens of stocks every day is essentially gambling. If you make some bad trades — which is unbelievably easy to do — you can *lose* a lot of money. It's not a good way to get rich.

Instead, learn to invest for the long run. Choose good stocks with solid fundamentals and excellent leadership in industries that are primed for future growth. Then let your stock sit. Don't do anything with it. Let it weather the ups and downs. If you invest wisely, you should do very well over time.

A. Getting Acquainted with Different Investment Vehicles

1 Make sure you have a safety net. Holding some money in reserve is a good idea because (a) if you lose your investment you'll have something to fall back on, and it will allow you to be a bolder investor since you won't be worried about risking every penny you own.

Save between three and six months' worth of expenses. Call it your emergency fund, set aside for large, unexpected expenses (job loss, medical expenses, auto accident, etc.). This money should be in cash or some other form that's very conservative and immediately available.

Once you have an emergency fund established, you can start to save for your long-term goals, like buying a home, retirement, and college tuition.

If your employer offers a retirement plan, this is a great vehicle for saving, because it can save on your tax bill, and your employer may contribute money to match some of your own contributions, which amounts to "free" money for you.

If you don't have a retirement plan through your workplace, most employees are allowed to accumulate tax-deferred savings in a traditional IRA or a Roth IRA. If you are self-employed, you have options like a SEP-IRA or a "SIMPLE" IRA. Once you've determined the type of account(s) to set up, you can then choose specific investments to hold within them.

Get current on all your insurance policies. This includes auto, health, homeowners/renters, disability, and life insurance. With luck, you'll never need insurance, but it's nice to have in the event of a disaster.

2 Learn a little bit about stocks. This is what most people think of when they consider "investing." Put simply, a stock is a share in the ownership of a business, a publicly-held company. The stock itself is a claim on what the company owns — its assets and earnings. When you buy stock in a company, you are making yourself part-owner. If the company does well, the value of the stock will probably go up, and the company may pay you a "dividend," a reward for your investment. If the company does poorly, however, the stock will probably lose value.

The value of stock comes from public perception of its worth. That means the stock price is driven by what people *think* it's worth, and the price at which a stock is purchased or sold is whatever the market will bear, even if the underlying value (as measured by certain fundamentals) might suggest otherwise.

A stock price goes up when more people want to buy that stock than sell it. Stock prices go down when more people want to sell than buy. In order to sell a stock, you have to find someone willing to buy at the listed price. In order to buy stock, you have to find someone selling their stock at a price you like.

The job of a stockbroker is to pair up buyers and sellers.

"Stocks" can mean a lot of different things. For example, penny stocks are stocks that trade at relatively low prices, sometimes just pennies.

Various stocks are bundled into what's called an index, like the Dow Jones Industrials, which is a list of 30 high-performing stocks. An index is a useful indicator of the performance of the whole market.

3 Familiarize yourself with bonds. Bonds are issuances of debt, similar to an IOU. When you buy a bond, you're essentially lending someone money. The borrower ("issuer") agrees to pay back the money (the "principal") when the life ("term") of the loan has expired. The issuer also agrees to pay interest on the principal at a stated rate. The interest is the whole point of the investment. The term of the bond can range from months to years, at the end of which period the borrower pays back the principal in full.

Here's an example: You buy a five-year municipal bond for $10,000 with an interest rate of 2.35%. Thus, you lend the municipality $10,000. Each year the municipality pays you interest on your bond in the amount of 2.35% of $10,000, or $235. After five years the municipality pays back your $10,000. So you've made back your principal plus a profit of $1175 in interest (5 x $235).

Generally the longer the term of the bond, the higher the interest rate. If you're lending your money for a year, you probably won't get a high-interest rate, because one year is a relatively short period of risk. If you're going to lend your money and not expect it back for ten years, however, you will be compensated for the higher risk you're taking, and the interest rate will be higher. This illustrates an axiom in investing: **The higher the risk, the higher the return.**

4 Understand the commodities market. When you invest in something like a stock or a bond, you invest in the business represented by that security. The piece of paper you get is worthless, but what it promises is valuable. A commodity, on the other hand, is something of inherent value, something capable of satisfying a need or desire. Commodities include pork bellies (bacon), coffee beans, oil, natural gas, and potash, among many other items. The commodity itself is valuable, because people want and use it.

People often trade commodities by buying and selling "futures." A future is simply an agreement to buy or sell a commodity at a certain price sometime in the future.

Futures were originally used as a "hedging" technique by farmers. Here's a simple example of how it works: Farmer Joe grows avocados. The price of avocados, however, is typically volatile, meaning that it goes up and down a lot. At the beginning of the season, the wholesale price of avocados is $4 per bushel. If Farmer Joe has a bumper crop of avocados but the price of avocados drops to $2 per bushel in April at harvest, Farmer Joe may lose a lot of money.

Joe, in advance of harvest as insurance against such a loss, sells a futures contract to someone. The contract stipulates that the buyer of the contract agrees to buy all of Joe's avocados at $4 per bushel in April.

Now Joe has protection against a price drop. If the price of avocados goes up, he'll be fine because he can sell his avocados at the market price. If the price of avocados drops to $2, he can sell his avocados at $4 to the buyer of the contract and make more than other farmers who don't have a similar contract.

The buyer of a futures contract always hopes that the price of a commodity will go up beyond the futures price he paid. That way he can lock in a lower-than-market price. The seller hopes that the price of a commodity will go down. He can buy the commodity at low (market) prices and then sell it to the buyer at a higher-than-market price.

5 Know a bit about investing in property. Investing in real estate can be a risky but lucrative proposition. There are lots of ways you can invest in property. You can buy a house and become a landlord. You pocket the difference between what you pay on the mortgage and what the tenant pays you in rent. You can also flip homes. That means you buy a home in need of renovations, fix it up, and sell it as quickly as possible. Real estate can be a profitable vehicle for some, but it is not without substantial risk involving property maintenance and market value.

Other ways of gaining exposure to real estate include collateralized mortgage obligations (CMOs) and collateralized debt obligations (CDOs), which are mortgages that have been bundled into securitized instruments. These, however, are tools for sophisticated investors: their transparency and quality can vary greatly, as revealed during the 2008 downturn.

Some people think that home values are guaranteed to go up. History has shown otherwise: real estate values in most areas show very modest rates of return after accounting for costs such as maintenance, taxes, and insurance. As with many investments, real estate values do invariably rise if given enough time. If your time horizon is short, however, property ownership is not a guaranteed money-maker.

Property acquisition and disposal can be a lengthy and unpredictable process and should be viewed as a long-term, higher-risk proposition. It is not the type of investment that is appropriate if your time horizon is short and is certainly not a guaranteed investment.

6 Learn about mutual funds and exchange-traded funds (ETFs). Mutual funds and ETFs are similar investment vehicles in that each is a collection of many stocks and/or bonds (hundreds or thousands in some cases). Holding an individual security is a concentrated way of investing – the potential for gain or loss is tied to a single company – whereas holding a fund is a way to spread the risk across many companies, sectors or regions. Doing so can dampen the upside potential but also serves to protect against the downside risk.

Commodities exposure is usually achieved by holding futures contracts or a fund of futures contracts. Real estate can be held directly (by owning a home or investment property) or in a real estate investment trust (REIT) or REIT fund, which holds interests in a number of residential or commercial properties.

B. Mastering Investment Basics

1 Buy undervalued assets ("buy low, sell high"). If you're talking about stocks and other assets, you want to buy when the price is low and sell when the price is high. If you buy 100 shares of stock on January 1st for $5 per share, and you sell those same shares on December 31st for $7.25, you just made $225. That may seem a paltry sum, but when you're talking about buying and selling hundreds or even thousands of shares, it can really add up.

How do you tell if a stock is undervalued? You need to look at a company closely — its earnings growth, profit margins, its P/E ratio, and its dividend yield — instead of looking at just one aspect and making a decision based on a single ratio or a momentary drop in the stock's price.

The price-to-earnings ratio is a common way of determining if a stock is undervalued. It simply divides a company's share price by its earnings. For example, if Company X is trading at $5 per share, with earnings of $1 per share, its price-to-earnings ratio is 5. That is to say, the company is trading at five times its earnings. The lower this figure, the more undervalued the company may be. Typical P/E ratios range between 15 and 20, although ratios outside that range are not uncommon. Use P/E ratios as only one of many indications of a stock's worth.

Always compare a company to its peers. For example, assume you want to buy Company X. You can look at Company X's projected earnings growth, profit margins, and price-to-earnings ratio. You would then compare these figures to those of Company X's closest competitors. If Company X has better profit margins, better-projected earnings, and a lower price-to-earnings ratio, it may be a better buy.

Ask yourself some basic questions: What will the market be for this stock in the future? Will it look bleaker or better? What competitors does this company have, and what are their prospects? How will this company be able to earn money in the future? These should help you come to a better understanding of whether a company's stock is under- or over-valued.

2 Invest in companies that you understand. Perhaps you have some basic knowledge regarding some business or industry. Why not put that to use? Invest in companies or industries that you know, because you're more likely to understand revenue models and prospects for future success. Of course, never put all your eggs in one basket: investing in only one -- or a very few -- companies can be quite risky. However, wringing value out of a single industry (whose workings you understand) will increase your chances of being successful.

For example, you may hear plenty of positive news on a new technology stock. It is important to stay away until you understand the industry and how it works. The principle of investing in companies you understand was popularized by renowned investor Warren Buffett, who made billions of dollars sticking only with business models he understood and avoiding ones he did not.

3 Avoid buying on hope and selling on fear. It's very easy and too tempting to follow the crowd when investing. We often get caught up in what other people are doing and take it for granted that they know what they're talking about. Then we buy stocks just because *other* people buy them or sell them when *other* people do. Doing this is easy. Unfortunately, it's a good way to lose money. Invest in companies that you know and believe in — and tune out the hype — and you'll be fine.

When you buy a stock that everyone else has bought, you're buying something that's probably worth less than its price (which has probably risen in response to the recent demand). When the market corrects itself (drops), you could end up buying high and then selling low, just the opposite of what you want to do. Hoping that a stock will go up just because everyone else thinks it will is foolish.

When you sell a stock that everyone else is selling, you're selling something that may be worth more than its price (which likely has dropped because of all the selling). When the market corrects itself (rises), you've sold low and will have to buy high if you decide you want the stock back.

Fear of losses can prove to be a poor reason to dump a stock.

If you sell based on fear, you may protect yourself from further declines, but you may also miss out on a rebound. Just as you did not anticipate the decline, you will not be able to predict the rebound. Stocks have historically risen over long time frames, which is why holding on to them and not overreacting to short-term swings is important.

4 Know the effect of interest rates on bonds. **Bond prices and interest rates have an inverse relationship. When interest rates go up, bond prices go down. When interest rates go down, bond prices go up. Here's why:**

Interest rates on bonds normally reflect the prevailing market interest rate. Say you buy a bond with an interest rate of 3%. If interest rates on other investments then go up to 4% and you're stuck with a bond paying 3%, not many people would be willing to buy your bond from you when they can buy another bond that pays them 4% interest. For this reason, you would have to lower the price of your bond in order to sell it. The opposite situation applies when bond market rates are falling.

5 Diversify. **Diversifying your portfolio is one of the most important things that you can do because it diminishes your risk.** Think of it this way: If you were to invest $5 in each of 20 different companies, all of the companies would have to go out of business before you would lose all your money. If you invested the same $100 in just one company, only that company would have to fail for all your money to disappear. Thus, diversified investments "hedge" against each other and keep you from losing lots of money because of the poor performance of a few companies.

Diversify your portfolio not only with a good mix of stocks and bonds, but go further by buying shares in companies of different sizes in different industries and in different countries. Often when one class of investment performs poorly, another class performs nicely. It is very rare to see all asset classes declining at the same time.

Many believe a balanced or "moderate" portfolio is one made up of 60% stocks and 40% bonds. Thus, a more aggressive portfolio might have 80% stocks and 20% bonds, and a more conservative portfolio might have 70% bonds and 30% stocks. Some advisors will tell you that your portfolio's percentage of bonds should roughly match your age.

6 Invest for the long run. Choosing good-quality investments can take time and effort. Not everyone can do the research and keep up with the dynamics of all the companies being considered. Many people instead employ a "buy and hold" approach of weathering the storms rather than attempting to predict and avoid market downturns. This approach works for most in the long term but requires patience and discipline. There are some, however, who choose to try their hand at being a day-trader, which involves holding stocks for a very short time (hours, even minutes). Doing so, however, does not often lead to success over the long term for the following reasons:

Brokerage fees add up. Every time you buy or sell a stock, a middleman known as a broker takes a cut for connecting you with another trader. These fees can really add up if you're making a lot of trades every day, cutting into your profit and magnifying your losses.

Many try to predict what the market will do and some will get lucky on occasion by making some good calls (and will claim it wasn't *luck*), but research shows that this tactic does not typically succeed over the long term.

The stock market rises over the long term. From 1871 to 2014, the S&P 500's compound annual growth rate was 9.77%, a rate of return many investors would find attractive. The challenge is to stay invested long-term while weathering the ups and downs in order to achieve this average: the standard deviation for this period was 19.60%, which means some years saw returns as high as 29.37% while other years experienced losses as large as 9.83%. Set your sights on the long term, not the short. If you're worried about all the dips along the way, find a graphical representation of the stock market over the years, and hang it somewhere you can see whenever the market is undergoing its inevitable—and temporary—declines.

7 Consider whether or not to short sell. This can be a "hedging" strategy, but it can also amplify your risk, so it's really suitable only for experienced investors. The basic concept is as follows: Instead of betting that the price of a security is going to increase, "shorting" is a bet that the price will drop. When you short a stock (or bond or currency), your broker actually lends you shares without your having to pay for them. Then you hope the stock's price goes down. If it does, you "cover," meaning you buy the actual shares at the current (lower) price and give them to the broker. The difference between the amount credited to you in the beginning and the amount you pay at the end is your profit.

Short selling can be dangerous, however, because it's not easy to predict a drop in price. If you use shortening for the purpose of speculation, be prepared to get burned sometimes. If the stock's price were to go up instead of down, you would be forced to buy the stock at a *higher* price than what was credited to you initially. If, on the other hand, you use shortening as a way to hedge your losses, it can actually be a good form of insurance.

This is an advanced investment strategy, and you should generally avoid it unless you are an experienced investor with extensive knowledge of markets. Remember that while a stock can only drop to zero, it can rise indefinitely, meaning that you could lose enormous sums of money through short-selling.

C. Starting out

1 Choose where to open your account. There are different options available: you can go to a brokerage firm (sometimes also called a warehouse or custodian) such as Fidelity, Charles Schwab or TD Ameritrade. You can open an account on the website of one of these institutions, or visit a local branch and choose to direct the investments on your own or pay to work with a staff advisor. You can also go directly to a fund company such as Vanguard, Fidelity, or T. Rowe Price and let them be your broker. They will offer you their own funds, of course, but many fund companies (such as the three just named) offer

platforms on which you can buy the funds of other companies, too. See below for additional options in finding an advisor.

Always be mindful of fees and minimum-investment rules before opening an account. Brokers all charge fees per trade (ranging from $4.95 to $10 generally), and may require a minimum initial investment (ranging from $500 to much higher).

Online brokers with no minimum initial investment requirements include Capital One Investing, TD Ameritrade, First Trade, TradeKing, and Options House.

If you want more help with your investing, there is a variety of ways to find financial advice: if you want someone who helps you in a non-sales environment, you can find an advisor in your area at one of the following sites: letsmakeaplan.org, www.napfa.org, and garrettplanningnetwork.com. You can also go to your local bank or financial institution. Many of these charge higher fees, however, and may require a large opening investment.

Some advisors (like Certified Financial Planners™) have the ability to give advice in a number of areas such as investments, taxes, and retirement planning, while others can only act on a client's instructions but not give advice, It's also important to know that not all people who work at financial institutions are bound to the "fiduciary" duty of putting a client's interests first. Before starting to work with someone, ask about their training and expertise to make sure they are the right fit for you.

2 Invest in a Roth IRA as soon in your working career as possible. If you're earning taxable income and you're at least 18, you can establish a Roth IRA. This is a retirement account to which you can contribute up to an IRS-determined maximum each year (the latest limit is the lesser of $5,500 or the amount earned plus an additional $1,000 "catch up" contribution for

those age 50 or older). This money gets invested and begins to grow. A Roth IRA can be a very effective way to save for retirement.

You don't get a tax deduction on the amount you contribute to a Roth, as you would if you contributed to a traditional IRA. However, any growth on top of the contribution is tax-free and can be withdrawn without penalty after you turn age 59½ (or earlier if you meet one of the exceptions to the age 59½ rule).

Investing as soon as possible in a Roth IRA is important. The earlier you begin investing, the more time your investment has to grow. If you invest just $20,000 in a Roth IRA before you're 30 years old and then stop adding any more money to it, by the time you're 72 you'll have a $1,280,000 investment (assuming a 10% rate of return). This example is merely illustrative. Don't stop investing at 30. Keep adding to your account. You will have a *very* comfortable retirement if you do.

How can a Roth IRA grow like this? By compound interest. The return on your investment, as well as reinvested interest, dividends, and capital gains, are added to your original investment such that any given rate of return will produce a larger profit through accelerated growth. If you are earning an average compound annual rate of return of 7.2%, your money will double in ten years. (This is known as "the rule of 72.")

You can open a Roth IRA through most online brokers as well as through most banks. If you are using a self-directed online broker, you will simply select a Roth IRA as the type of account while you are registering.

3 Invest in your company's 401(k). A 401(k) is a retirement-savings vehicle into which an employee can direct portions of his or her paychecks and receive a tax deduction in the year of the contributions. Many employers will match a portion of

these contributions, so the employee should contribute at least enough to trigger the employer match.

4 Consider investing mainly in stocks but also in bonds to diversify your portfolio. From 1925 to 2011, stocks outperformed bonds in every rolling 25-year period. While this may sound appealing from a return standpoint, it entails volatility, which can be worrisome. Add less-volatile bonds to your portfolio for the sake of stability and diversification. The older you get, the more appropriate it becomes to own bonds (a more conservative investment). Reread the above discussion of diversification

5 Start off investing a little money in mutual funds. An index fund is a mutual fund that invests in a specific list of companies of a particular size or economic sector. Such a fund performs similarly to its index, such as the S&P 500 index or the Barclays Aggregate Bond index.

Mutual funds come in different shapes and sizes. Some are actively managed, meaning there is a team of analysts and other experts employed by the fund company to research and understand a particular geographical region or economic sector. Because of this professional management, such funds generally cost more than index funds, which simply mimic an index and don't need much management. They can be bond-heavy, stock-heavy, or invest in stocks and bonds equally. They can buy and sell their securities actively, or they can be more passively managed (as in the case of index funds).

Mutual funds come with fees. There may be charges (or "loads") when you buy or sell shares of the fund. The fund's "expense ratio" is expressed as a percentage of total assets and pays for overhead and management expenses. Some funds charge a lower-percentage fee for larger investments. Expense ratios generally range from as low as 0.15% (or 15 basis points, abbreviated "BPS") for index funds to as high as 2% (200 BPS) for actively managed funds. There may also be a "12b-1" fee charged to offset a fund's marketing expenses.

The U.S. Securities and Exchange Commission states that no evidence exists that higher-fee mutual funds produce better returns than do lower-fee funds. In other words, deal with lower-fee funds.

Mutual funds can be purchased through nearly any brokerage service. Even better is to purchase directly from a mutual fund company. This avoids brokerage fees. Call or write the fund company or visit their website. Opening a fund account is simple and easy. See Invest in Mutual Funds.

6 Consider exchange-traded funds in addition to or instead of mutual funds. Exchange-traded funds (ETFs) are very similar to mutual funds in that they pool people's money and buy many investments. There are a few key differences:

ETFs can be traded on an exchange throughout the business day just like stocks, whereas mutual funds are bought and sold only at the end of each trading day.

ETFs are typically index funds and do not generate as much in the way of taxable capital gains to pass on to investors as compared with actively managed funds. ETFs and mutual funds are becoming less distinct from each other, and investors need not own both types of investment. If you like the idea of buying and selling fund shares during (rather than at the end of) the trading day, ETFs are a good choice for you.

D. Making the Most of Your Money

1 Consider using the services of a financial planner or advisor. Many planners and advisors require that their clients have an investment portfolio of at least a minimum value, sometimes $100,000 or more. This means it could be hard to find an advisor willing to work with you if your portfolio isn't

well established. In that case, look for an advisor interested in helping smaller investors.

How do financial planners help? Planners are professionals whose job is to invest your money for you, ensure that your money is safe, and guide you in your financial decisions. They draw from a wealth of experience at allocating resources. Most importantly, they have a financial stake in your success: the more money you make under their tutelage, the more money they make.

2 Buck the herd instinct. **The herd instinct, alluded to earlier, is the idea that just because a lot of other people are doing something, you should, too. Many successful investors have made moves that the majority thought was unwise at the time.**

That doesn't mean, however, that you should never seek investment advice from other people. Just be wise about choosing the people you listen to. Friends or family members with a successful background in investing can offer worthwhile advice, as can professional advisors who charge a flat fee (rather than a commission) for their help.

Invest in smart opportunities when other people are scared. In 2008 as the housing crisis hit, the stock market shed thousands of points in a matter of months. A smart investor who bought stocks as the market bottomed out enjoyed a strong return when stocks rebounded.

This reminds us to buy low and sell high. It takes courage to buy investments when they are becoming cheaper (in a falling market) and sell those investments when they are looking better and better (a rising market). It seems counter-intuitive, but it's how the world's most successful investors made their money.

3 Know the players in the game. **Which institutional investors think that your stock is going to drop in price and have therefore shorted it? What mutual fund managers have your**

stock in their fund, and what is their track record? While it helps to be independent as an investor, it's also helpful to know what respected professionals are doing.

There are websites that compile recent opinions on a stock from analysts and expert investors. For example, if you are considering a purchase of Tesla shares, you can search Tesla on the Stock chase. It will give you all the recent expert opinions on the stock.

4 Re-examine your investment goals and strategies every so often. Your life and conditions in the market change all the time, so your investment strategy should change with them. Never be so committed to a stock or bond that you can't see it for what it's worth.

While money and prestige may be important, never lose track of the truly important, non-material things in life: your family, friends, health, and happiness.

For example, if you are very young and saving for retirement, it may be appropriate to have most of your portfolio invested in stocks or stock funds. This is because you would have a longer time horizon in which to recover from any big market crashes or declines, and you would be able to benefit from the long-term trend of markets moving higher.

If you are just about to retire, however, having much less of your portfolio in stocks, and a large portion in bonds and/or cash equivalents is wise. This is because you will need the money in the short-term, and as a result, you do not want to risk losing the money in a stock market crash right before you need it.

Save money for retirement.

Keep saving. It seems that fewer people are saving adequately for retirement. Some feel they may never be able to retire. Take advantage of tax-deferred retirement plans such as IRAs and 401Ks. The tax treatment they embody will help you save faster for retirement.

Don't put all your trust in Social Security. While it's a good bet that Social Security will continue to work for the next 20 or so years, some data suggest that if Congress doesn't radically alter the system — either by raising taxes or reducing benefits — Social Security won't be available in its current form. It is probable; however, that Congress will act to "fix" Social Security. In any event, Social Security was never designed to be the only resource for retirees in their later years. That makes it all the more important that you save and invest for the future.

Invest in a Roth IRA. A Roth IRA is a retirement account to which working individuals can contribute an annual sum of $5,500. That money is then invested and gathers compound interest. If you wait until retirement age to take money out of your Roth IRA, the money that you withdraw isn't taxed, because it was taxed at the time you first earned it.

Contribute to a 401(k) account. This is an account set up by your employer where pre-taxed contributions can be invested. Your employer may choose to match all or part of your contributions. This is probably the closest thing you'll get to "free money" in your life! Contribute at least enough to take full advantage of the match.

Basic steps:

1 Seek the advice of professional financial advisors to help you with this task, realizing you can't afford to make mistakes since you'll need to make every dollar grow. **Saving and investing for**

a reliable retirement income for the rest of your life — no matter how long you live — is an ambitious undertaking that takes knowledge, time and skill. So, it's likely that you may need or want this kind of help.

That said good advice does not have to cost you anything other than time. Plenty of excellent books on retirement savings are freely available for you to read courtesy of your local public library. Try to be discerning though, and check the reviews available online such as from Amazon.com. While some books are worth their weight in gold, others are drivels worth far less than zero.

Take free online financial classes such as from Coursera.org and MIT Open Courseware. Your local college may also offer financial classes you can audit for free.

Don't hand over your money for a financial advisor to manage. At best, you will be charged a 1% asset under management (AUM) fee that would cost you about one-third of what you could have after 40 years, assuming a 7 percent return per year. (I.e. if you start with $100,000, instead of having $1.5 million after 40 years, you would end up with only $1.0 million, paying half a million to your financial adviser alone, while you assumed all the risk associated with investing.) At worst, most or all your money may be stolen by an unscrupulous financial advisor.

If you still feel you need a personal financial advisor, go with a fee-only advisor (NOT "fee-based"!!) with no adverse action on record and who will contain costs by choosing low-cost broad market-based index funds with low turnover. Even with a very small portfolio, don't agree to more than 1% AUM fee. And if you have a large portfolio, you should be able to negotiate fees down to 0.5% or less.

2 Budget to save as much money as possible and avoid unnecessary spending. **A good, aggressive saving goal should be**

at least 50% of your after-tax earnings. Cut down on luxuries. Don't spend "seed" money but invest/germinate the seeds, hold/plant and water--nor do you "eat nest eggs" that need to be allowed to "hatch," grow and multiply into a productive "flock" of investments. Live mostly on absolute essentials, (food, shelter, transportation)... Search around for the best prices. Buy things that will appreciate in value (e.g.: a home, collectible gold, land, rentals [renters buy "their" houses/apartments "for you", and pay the repairs, insurance, and taxes but those expenses are deductible]...) and avoid things that depreciate in value (e.g.: a new, or expensive car, big TVs). For example, read books or watch basic television channels instead of paying for cable television, cook your own food instead of dining in restaurants, and quit smoking. Learn to live simply on modest means, and always look for free or economical alternatives. Always think of opportunity cost: the dollar you spend now could have turned into many dollars by the time you retire. Smart spending will provide the foundation for saving money for retirement.

3 If you live in the United States and it is available to you, enroll in a 401(k) account. If your employer offers 100% match up to a maximum that will be matched, find out what the maximum is, and contribute at least the amount required to get the maximum company match. 401(k) accounts are actually mutual funds that can charge high fees (e.g. around 1% per year), and therefore will not do as well as investing in stocks and bonds directly. But, with an employer matching your funds, you can double your investment immediately, and then hopefully your fund investment will increase in value. 401(k) accounts also offer tax advantages; inquire and read about them. You may be required to contribute at least a minimum amount to qualify for employer matching (to save about 10-30% of your income). Remember that 401k's are taxed upon distribution; so try to estimate what the tax rate will be when you take your money out. Estimate your tax before using withdrawn money; you need to hold back enough for paying those taxes.

4 Develop an investment plan known as a portfolio for your saved money. A portion should be delegated to stocks, another portion to bonds, perhaps another portion to commodities like gold and silver, and another portion to cash in the form of savings account, certificates of deposit (CDs), etc. If you are not near retirement, an example allocation is 60% stocks, 20% bonds, 10% gold and silver, 10% cash. The reason for diversification is to reduce risks and maximize returns. By not having all assets in a single asset, you are less affected -- if the value of one component of your portfolio crashes.

5 Rebalance the categories in your portfolio periodically (e.g. monthly, quarterly, or annually) to maintain the proportions. For the example above, if stocks crash and gold and silver soar, the weight of stocks will be less than 60% and gold and silver more than 10%. You will then sell gold and silver to buy stocks until 60% stocks (unless you are near retirement) and 10% gold and silver are restored. Rebalancing helps you to maintain control of your emotions and *practice buying low and selling high*, rather than the reverse. This will help you lower the risks of losing money.

To minimize transaction costs, you should rebalance by predominantly adding new money to under-weighted assets during your wealth accumulation stage, and selling over-weighted assets during your wealth distribution stage.

6 Diversify within each asset class of your portfolio by assigning a weight to each subclass. Buy stocks both domestic and foreign, from every sector, and of any market cap. Buy both government and corporate bonds. As for gold and silver, buy physical metals to take possession. Don't trust others to store your valuables for you that you bought at high costs. Don't buy gold and silver more than 10-15% over the spot, or else they would have to appreciate a lot for you not to lose money when you need to cash out. Gold and silver coins over 100 years old may be considered better than bullion because they have numismatic value in addition to their intrinsic metal values.

7 Consider changing your assets into a form such as life annuity where you could not lose it, if you are sued whether you have too much to lose or just enough to tempt a swindler. You can be certain that some people like to try to pickpockets that have discoverable assets. Attorneys of anyone who may sue you will use *compulsory discovery processes* and you can be required to reveal your assets. Avoid seeing your life savings go to other accounts. Also, purchasing "umbrella" liability insurance for more protection may be a good plan. Your insurance agent will tell you your options and how much you should get.

8 Reduce risk when nearing retirement and stay out of high risks from that time on. Reduce the portion in your portfolio delegated to risks such as stocks and increase the portion in safe investments including municipal bonds and cash. Chances are, the market will decline or even may crash when you need to be taking out your money. What can go wrong includes not having the time or opportunity to recoup losses from dire events in the market, and you might have to postpones retirement-if you did not reduce your risks to the minimum

A. Accelerate Retirement Savings According to Your Age

1 Follow these general guidelines to help you build your retirement savings depending on the number of years until you would retire. The percentages to invest assume you are just beginning to save and have the goal of maintaining your lifestyle for up to 30 years of retirement.

2 If you start saving in your 20s:

Save between 10 percent and 15 percent of your income for your retirement investments.

Do not cut back on your retirement savings.

Small contributions to your retirement plan can grow over time.

3 If you start saving in your 30s:

Save between 15 percent and 25 percent of your income for your retirement investments.

Keep a list of your spending to find ways that you may see to cut back.

If you receive a bonus, put as much of it as possible into your retirement savings.

Also, fund your retirement accounts -- even if you begin saving for your children's college expenses, or even if you pay extra on your mortgage to pay it off early.

4 If you start saving in your early 40s:
Save between 25 percent and 35 percent of your income for your retirement investments.

Put the maximum amount into your 401(k), SEP-IRA, or other retirement plans at your place of employment.

Contribute to a traditional IRA (or Roth IRA, if eligible).

Consider a deferred variable annuity is another option.

Consider less expensive public (state) universities for your children, or ask that they use educational loans, grants, and scholarships.

5 If you start saving in your mid-40s and older:

Save more than 35 percent of your income for your retirement investments.

Put the maximum amount into all of your tax-deferred retirement account options.

6 Get out of "risk-based" investments by your early fifties: About 10 years before your planned retirement age, put all funds in fixed income, "safe" investments. At 50 years of age there would be no time to recover from a market crash or a sharp downturn, so it is time to put money in guaranteed returns.

B. Consider Income-only versus Income & Growth Options

1 Consider income-only products. You should read prospectus documents. Do not make any decisions under pressure or on the whim of the moment. Check with as many companies as you like. Take your time to decide:

"Bonds" may give fixed earnings. You can choose taxable, or tax-free interest payouts, and use bond laddering (bonds becoming mature at different times) to stabilize your income.

"Bond mutual funds" which are made of a number of bonds may create a periodic payout with bond mutual funds. Some brokers can give you choices with screening of shortlists of tax-free and taxable bond funds that they recommend (sell).

"CDs" may be competitively priced CDs that offer a fixed interest payout from FDIC-insured banks nationwide.

"Income annuities" are used to secure a guaranteed income stream throughout your life that's independent of interest rate changes or market volatility with an income annuity.

"Income mutual funds": Identify no-transaction-fee funds that emphasize income distributions while still providing growth potential to help you keep pace with the cost of living. Choose from funds designed to produce monthly payments of investment income while giving your savings opportunity to grow. Monthly Income Funds give you a range of options to match your targeted income needs.

"Variable annuities" may have guaranteed lifetime withdrawal benefits. There are annuity investments with the option of a guaranteed monthly lifetime income.

C. Tips

It is easier to save for retirement if you work for employers who offer the best benefits, such as retirement plan match, tuition reimbursement, pensions, or even health care for retirees.

If you have a 401(k) and left the job, you may choose to keep the money with your old employer, provided you have at least $5000 in the account (this is typically the best option; you can always move it later if you want), or roll it into an IRA if you want more investment options. You can also cash it out, but this is typically ill-advised, as you could lose nearly half of your account balance to taxes and early-withdrawal penalties.

Consider Individual Retirement Accounts (IRA), if you live in the United States. They may offer some tax benefits. The caveat is that you cannot withdraw money from IRAs or another standard retirement plan without paying a hefty penalty until you reach 59 1/2 years old.

Please note that 401(k) and IRA accounts are available only in the United States. They are passive ways to invest your savings for retirement with some tax benefits. If you live outside the United States, simply follow the steps as above to save for your retirement and manage your money actively.

Diversify away from what you already have. For example, if you have a steady job, it is like a huge bond that pays distribution every month, in which case you should buy more stocks than bonds.

Develop a well-diversified portfolio and keep it in line with the proportion that you have set. This will motivate you to buy low (in a crashed category) and sell high (in a booming category) while keeping emotions to a minimum and with a cool mind.

If you have high-risk tolerance and a very long investment horizon (i.e. you won't need the money for at least 20 years), consider putting it 100% into stocks, or even using a little leverage, by going on margin (leverage under 1.5 should be pretty safe, and under no circumstance should you go beyond 2:1 leverage, or else you would be tempting fate).

Saving money for retirement is a life-long commitment and investment. It is important to put aside money for this end regularly.

It is never too early to start saving for retirement. The earlier you start, the more savings you will have, and the easier it will be if you develop the habit of saving early on. You will accumulate more wealth for retirement, if you start saving sooner, and let compounding interest work for you. On the other hand, it is never too late to save for retirement. Start where you are and do your best.

Save money separately for emergencies such as a loss of income.

Don't ever use any of your retirement savings unless it is really needed.

D. Warnings

Keep your head cool. Don't chase hot stocks, and don't panic when stocks drop. The worst thing you can do to lose money fast is to be overly enthusiastic when the market rises and buy high, and sell low when the market declines. This is why it is critically important to develop a well-diversified portfolio and stick to it by rebalancing regularly.

Avoid double risk by investing heavily in the economic sector that pays your paycheck. For example, if you work in the financial sector, and your portfolio is heavy in financial stocks, you could risk losing both your job and your savings when the financial sector of the economy crashes. Diversification is the key to risk reduction.

Be wary of high fees that can eat away your return, such as those charged by actively managed mutual funds, financial advisors, and many annuity products.

Never take on credit card debts, unless you are taking advantage of a 0% introductory APR offer and paying the balance in full when the introductory period is over. Do not use credit cards at all unless you can be sure to pay off the entire sum every month. Learn to build credit without credit cards. Buy only essential things, and use the money you already have, not money you expect to have.

The most important thing is to start saving for retirement early!! If you save $100 a month starting at age 20, you will have $1,048,250 at age 65, assuming 10% annual return. But if you waited till age 30, saving the same $100 a month will provide you with only $379,664 at age 65. Much of the return is due to compound interest from the savings when you were young. That is why compound interest is called the eighth wonder of the world.

Investing is different from speculation. Your saving for retirement is not risk capital. Don't buy into promises of fast money with hot stock picks or the forex market. Stocks that are hot will burn your retirement money. The forex market is played by professionals with many years of experience and is entirely speculation, inappropriate for any money designated for retirement.

Many people lost 50% or more of their investments in stocks, bonds, and the highly leveraged real estate bubble around the year 2008. There were similar devastating events in the 1970s. Also, in the 1980s and 90s savings and loan (S&L) crisis, more than 1600 of about 3200 of these "fixed" real estate income investments failed, as over-leveraged institutions went bankrupt. Some funds were insured by the Federal FSLIC, but some were not insured. There were similar high-risk loans and failures during the 2007 subprime mortgage financial crisis in real estate mortgages. One day such seemingly viable/safe investments are up -- but virtually the next day the market is through the floor, and funds disintegrate as into ether (vapor).

E.   Inflation Warning

See how 7% inflation nearly doubles the cost of living in 10 years: ($1.07^{10}=1.96$). That is about 2X (two times) cost, for example, if a gallon of milk did cost $3, it would cost nearly $6, 10 years later and the then $6 milk would cost $12 after 20 years. Inflation *slashes* funds from availability for saving and *encourages* spending by necessity.

Expect wages and salary to lag behind as companies must also deal with the inflation in every area of its costs. This, in turn, leads to higher costs of investment as the value of your dollars saved is shrinking since you need an increase of 7% or more dollars every year to just keep up with the inflation. When the price level rises, each dollar buys fewer goods and services -- a real loss of value:

If you borrow funds, (with an excellent credit rating, at an interest rate of 8% when there is extremely low inflation), but now assume 7% inflation.

If you save money at the interest rate of 3% and the business firm could borrow it from the bank at 8%. The profit margin to the bank is 5% each year, but inflation would destroy that possibility.

Account for inflation of 7%, however, as the bank is likely to need to increase the cost of borrowing from 8% by adding 7% to make that about 15% which is nearly 100% higher to cover the cost of inflation.

Caution: Less than perfect credit could double the rates or make credit unavailable.

Invest in real estate.

Relatively stable assets like rental properties or potential development land in a steadily growing area is a good way to build wealth. As with any investment, there are no guarantees. Many people, however, have done quite well with real estate. Such investments are likely to appreciate in value over time. For example, some people think that an apartment in Manhattan is almost guaranteed to increase in value over any five-year period

When you invest in residential real estate, you are getting more than a home or a piece of land upon which to build a home. Real estate investment has become a popular way for people to make money, and it is not uncommon to buy a house or land without any intention of living there. Some people simply buy and hold property, waiting for it to appreciate in value before reselling it. Having cash for a down payment is the quick and easy way to enter the real estate market, but it's not your only option. Many people have found ways to start investing in real estate with little or no money of their own. Options include borrowing money as well as a number of more unusual and creative paths to ownership.

A.   Investing Without a Down Payment

1 Look into seller financing. If the seller is motivated enough, s/he may be willing to make it easy for you to purchase by giving you a loan. You could offer to make higher monthly payments instead of a down payment.

You could also negotiate a deal where the seller pays your down payment to a traditional lender in order to sell the property faster. The seller might expect you to pay him/her back or s/he may throw the down payment in for free, essentially lowering the selling price.

For each of these scenarios, make sure you have a real estate attorney write up the agreement so that both parties are protected.

2 Lease the property with the option to buy. You can invest in real estate slowly by making payments on a lease agreement until you have the money to buy. Your payments would (at least in part) be credited toward the purchase price.

Ensure the agreement specifically states a final price for the property. Define the exact portion of the rental payments that will be put toward the final purchase price.

3 Work out a trade. You can pay for real estate by bartering another piece of property or a specialized skill you have. For example, a contractor could offer a real estate developer labor in exchange for a down payment.

Other possessions you could offer to swap include motor homes, campers, boats, cars, large appliances, valuable artwork, and furniture.

For any bartering deal, draw up a legal agreement with an attorney specifically stating the value of each item in the trade. An outside appraisal may be needed.

4 Take over mortgage payments. If you are interested in investing in a piece of real estate but you can't afford the down payment, offer to take over the mortgage payments in exchange for the deed. However, you will need to investigate the existing loan before you make such an offer. Some mortgage loans have specific language preventing this type of transaction.

You could also offer to take over a seller's other debts such as credit card payments instead of a down payment. This is something you could pay off over time. Put the agreement in writing, as if you don't pay the credit cards on time the seller's credit rating will be negatively affected

B. Co-Investing for a Down Payment

1 Bring in a partner. If you are big on ideas but short on cash, bringing in a partner who will provide the funding and allow you to do the managing might be an attractive option. You will need to write up a contract that establishes who is responsible for what, and how the profits will be divided.

If your partner is in place strictly for financial support, make sure you retain all control over the day-to-day management of your investment.

2 Invest with a building contractor. If you lack carpentry, plumbing and electrical skills to fix up and resell a property, partner with someone who does have these skills and could help with the down payment. Once you make a profit on the sale, you will have the down payment for your next real estate investment.

C. Borrowing Money for a Down Payment

1 Borrow money from family or friends. If you have little or no money on hand and you want to make a real estate investment, borrowing money from family and friends is another option. Be sure to write up an official promissory note with payment due dates, a specific interest rate, and what ownership, if any, the lender will have in the property. If you pay back the loan on time and with interest, these lenders might be willing to lend to you again for future projects.

Consider whether the relationship you have with your lender could be harmed if you were unable to repay the loan. Ask yourself if securing real estate is worth endangering your relationship with someone close to you.

2 Take out a home equity loan. Find a bank that will allow you to take out a loan for a down payment on top of the mortgage loan you have on your own house. This could be a line of credit or a second mortgage using your home as collateral. Look for a low-interest rate that will allow you to purchase the property economically enough that you can still make a profit later on your investment.

Make sure you can pay back this loan or you risk losing your own home. You will also have to have a credit score in the high 600s to take out this type of loan.

3 Consider a micro lender. Internet micro lending services (also called peer to peer lending) help borrowers find lenders for relatively small loans, usually under $35,000. Research these sites and familiarize yourself with all of the rules and regulations in order to avoid misunderstandings later.

Popular micro lending sites include Kiva, Prosper, and Lending Club.

D. Finding Properties to Purchase

1 Work with an experienced real estate broker. It will cost you nothing to work with a real estate broker experienced in finding properties that have the potential of not requiring a down payment. Ask people experienced in real estate investing for names of brokers they have worked with. Look for details about a particular agent's background on the real estate company's website.

2 Seek out, motivated sellers. These people are desperate to sell for reasons such as bankruptcy, divorce, death of a relative, an out-of-town new job, poor condition of the property, behind on payments, etc. They will be more open to providing funding to close the deal quickly. Your local real estate broker can help provide information on who might be in this situation.

3 Search online for properties that offer incentives. These can include little or no down payment or seller financing. Check out

homepath.com, a resale marketing site. Fannie Mae also lists thousands of properties they acquired through foreclosure.

Invest your time.

For example, you might like having free time, so you give yourself a few hours a day to do nothing. But if you were to invest those few hours into getting rich, you could work towards having 20 years of free time (24 hours a day!) with early retirement. What can you give up now in exchange for being rich later? Investment advisor Dave Ramsey likes to tell his radio audience, "Live like no one else today so that you can live like no one else tomorrow."

1 Invest in "Life-Extending" Time. Investing time in caring for your health is an obvious one that will certainly yield you more time, literally—in days, months, if not years tacked on to your life. Yet we often take our health for granted until we experience a wake-up call. Proactively invest your time in your health by eating well, exercising regularly, getting plenty of sleep, and regularly seeing your doctors. Invest heartily in those non-physical markers of well-being as well: emotional, mental, and spiritual health—you will reap many hours of well-lived life from them. Learn the habits of the Blue Zone people, from the regions in the world where people live the longest. Some common lifestyle traits they share? Building in natural movement and activity, lowering stress, and being part of a faith-based community.

2 Invest in "Foundation-Building" Time. There's a little saying that goes, "a stitch in time saves nine." Create the time to make the right stitches, and you'll be spared much time, hassle, and usually expense later. Stephen Covey refers to this concept in The 7 Habits of Highly Effective People. According to him, we spend our time primarily on four types of activity:

Urgent and important (crisis, deadlines, putting out fires)

Non-urgent and important (building relationships, identifying opportunities, prevention, planning)

Urgent and non-important (interruptions, phone calls, meetings)

Non-urgent and non-important (TV, email, time wasters)

Covey says that we spend most of our time in sections 1 and 4, but the real area of personal growth is in 2. If you're spending more time putting out fires than building the right foundations, you'll never get out ahead of your to-do list.

3 Invest in "Do-Nothing" Time. Americans could use a little dose of "La Dolce Far Niente," or "the sweetness of doing nothing," something the Italians and many other cultures have mastered. In America, we don't feel our time is well spent unless we're either producing or consuming, says social psychologist Robert V. Levine, author of A Geography of Time: On Tempo, Culture, and the Pace of Life, which is a limited (and frankly, stressful) perspective. In other parts of the world, such as India, it's normal for people to enjoy each other's company without activity or even conversation. Investing in do-nothing time will help us slow down and experience a different pace of life, in which time's value is not measured by its productivity.

4 Invest in "System-Creating" Time. It's well-established in happiness psychology research that making small improvements to your life pays out exponentially in happiness. For example, putting a key hook by the door so that you don't spend five minutes every morning hunting for your keys. Or rearranging your closet so you can actually see everything, and not spend 20 minutes each morning figuring out what to wear. Or coming up with a better filing system for your digital photos, or your expenses (check out Learn Vest's My Money Center), so your personal admin time can be cut in half. Investing some up-front time in creating better, more organized systems will reap you lots of time in the long run.

5 Invest in "Cushion" Time. This is one of those time investments that are so simple but can yield such great results

in your life. In the famous "Good Samaritan" study from Princeton University in 1973, researchers John M. Darley and C. Daniel Batson put an injured person in the path of several groups of people, to see who would stop and help: those running late, those who had just enough time, and those with plenty of time to get to their destination. They also controlled for people's religious affiliation. The results: religious affiliation had no impact on whether the individual stopped to help the person—but whether the person was in a hurry had a huge impact. Only 10% of those in a big hurry stopped to help the person, 45% of those in a medium hurry did—but 63% of those not rushed at all stopped to help. This means that being in a rush may be preventing you from being the kind of person you want to be—the kind to stop and help someone in need. Building in lots of cushion time in your schedule and preventing "constant hurriedness syndrome" is a great investment in yourself and in the quality of life of those around you.

6 Invest in "Savoring" Time. A recent 2010 study published in the Association for Psychological Science found that wealthy people are unhappier because they have a lower "savoring ability" (the ability to enhance and prolong positive emotional experience), like taking in the colors of a sunset or the taste of a cold beer. Apparently, having access to the best things in life may actually undermine your ability to reap enjoyment from life's small pleasures. It's not a coincidence that savoring requires slowing down—taking a few extra seconds to really look at the colors of the leaves, or munching slowly to enjoy the texture of a bite. Investing time in savoring all the unique sensorial moments of your day will guarantee your moments don't flash by in a dull blur.

7 Invest in "Time Assessment" Time. You wouldn't keep spending or investing money without assessing how well things were going every month, quarter, or year, and the same thing should apply to your time. How frequently you decide to take stock is up to you—but a good system might be:

Five minutes a day to make sure you've invested time in at least one thing on this list.

15 minutes a week to review your past week's schedule and what you wish you had made time for, and what time investment made you happiest.

One hour a month (or two to three hours a season) of quiet time with a journal to assess the past season, how your time felt, and how you'd like to invest your time in the coming season—this can pair nicely with the tempo of the period. For example, holidays may mean more family investment time, the New Year can be career-focused, and summertime may have a big leisure time component.

One day a year of time alone or with a friend or partner (best if you can physically go somewhere peaceful and different from your daily routine), assessing the past year and where your times and energies went, setting goals for the new year, and whether you are closer to achieving what is truly important to you in life.

Avoid purchases that are likely to depreciate rapidly.

Spending $50,000 on a car is sometimes considered a waste because it's likely that it won't be worth half that much in five years, regardless of how much work you put into it. As soon as you drive a new car off the lot, it depreciates about 20%-25% in value and continues to do so each year you own it. That makes buying a car a very important financial decision.

- ## Basic steps:

1 Decide upon your needs. Learn to live with less. Layer your summer clothes during the winter for a different look. Learn to use a small purse. Limit makeup and accessories. Going without can be a real adventure

2 Make your own style. Start an inexpensive, unconventional trend. Ignore advertising. Why follow the crowd?

3 Have style. Choose your outfits carefully. Look for the most accentuating outfits worn by others with the same figure, skin tone, or hair color. Wearing different shades of the same color is slimming and easy to put together.

4 Extend your wardrobe. Take the time to coordinate your clothes into a month's worth of outfits. Make a list of all possible combinations and refer to it frequently.

5 Make a plan. Determine what you need to complete any outfit. Something that doesn't match or fit well may never be worn.

6 Be sure it's exceptional. Be patient. Check for quality, color, fit and a long-lasting style. You'll want to wear a garment for a few seasons, then recycle the fabric into another garment or accessory.

7 Compare clearance prices online. Have a rough idea of what you're willing to pay. Review the current styles. Keep a list of reasonable prices in your purse.

8 Try the flea market. You'll find a variety of unique imported and second-hand items. You can bargain for a better price.

9 Try the dollar store. Their selection may be limited, but they have cute clothes and accessories. This is a great place to buy pajamas and slippers.

10 Try thrift stores. Vintage is always in fashion. Brand names can be found. Worn clothing is very comfortable. Look for fabrics to make something new.

11 Try Walmart. Search both the men's and women's departments. If you're petite, search the children's department as well. This is a great place for the basics.

12 Try Target. They have a stylish clothing line of good quality and reasonable prices.

13 Watch for sales. Use coupons during the holiday sales, either online or in stores. Try things on prior to a sale. Take time to think things over to avoid impulse shopping.

14 Bring a limited amount of cash. Stay within your budget. Leave credit cards at home.

15 Do not remove the tags. Wait a week to think it over. Remove the tags once you're sure you'll enjoy your new item.

16 Check a lot of shops before buying anything. Usually a lot of shops have the same things, so you should check before buying. You'll probably find clothes that look alike for cheaper than in other stores.

17 Choose quality over quantity. Rather than buying 10 cheap shirts, go for one good quality shirt. Don't be careless while buying cosmetics. While buying new products buy the smallest packet or get a free sample for a trial run, if it suits you then go ahead.

- Tips

If your phone has the ability to, join every coupon app that you can find. This way whenever you walk into a store you can pull up a coupon for it.

Clothes should glide over your body whether sitting or standing. A larger size may be more appropriate.

Allow yourself to splurge on one small item.

Go straight to the clearance rack! If you do not find anything on that rack, look at the other clothes, but be sure you are getting your money's worth and are not burning a hole through your wallet.

Make a list before you shop. Write down what you need, and how much it costs for each part. Then you won't use too much money.

Don't spend money on stupid stuff.

It's hard enough making a living. But it's hard and painful when the things you spend your hard-earned cash on are financial black holes. Reevaluate the things you spend money on. Try to figure out whether they are truly "worth it." Here are some things you probably don't want to spend that much money on if you plan on becoming rich:

Casinos and lottery tickets. The lucky few make money. The rest of us lose it.

Vices such as cigarettes. Heavy smokers can only watch their money go up in smoke.

Huge markups like candy at the movie theatre or drinks at a club.

Tanning booths and plastic surgery. You can get skin cancer for free outside if you'd like. And do nose jobs and Botox injections ever look as good as promised? Learn how to age gracefully! You're not the only one getting older.

First-class plane tickets. What are you getting for that extra $1,000? A hot towel and another 4 inches (10.2 cm) of legroom? Invest that money instead of throwing it away.

▪ TOP 10 STUPID THINGS THAT WE WASTE MONEY ON

1   Fast Food. I know it's quick and I know how hard it is to find the time to cook at home. Trust me. We were addicted to fast food for years because I didn't know how to cook and we had awful organizational skills.

It took us a long time to learn to cook at home and we had to start with super simple 15-minute recipes to get us there. But the money that you will save is immense.

The money isn't even the best part! You'll eat so much better and you'll consume fewer calories, making you healthier and even happier.

2 Brand Name. Products We used to buy brand name everything even when we couldn't afford it. That makes me cringe now.

Even when we taste-tested, there were very few items for which the brand name items liked better. Most tasted exactly the same, and we often found a store brand that we liked better. The exception to this (and the only things we still buy in name brand) are Hellmann's mayonnaise and McIlhenny Chipotle Tabasco Sauce.

By switching to store brands in everything else, we automatically save about 30% off on our grocery bills without even noticing a difference.

3 Cable. This is usually the hardest for readers to try, but I've never had a single reader say they switched back to cable.

This was easy for us. We had an Xbox, so we just got Hulu for $7.99 and Netflix for $8.99/month and called it a day.

We saved $80/month, had better TV than when we had cable, and had the unexpected added benefit of never having to watch the news (I never realized how much stress the news caused until we lived without it).

There are so many options today for cheaper alternatives to cable that it boggles my mind that cable companies can still make a living.

4   In-App Purchases. It's not that these small purchases cost a lot, it's that they're so completely senseless.

Buying extra lives in angry birds, and candy crush is not only a waste of money (and your time!) but if you just put the phone down for 20 minutes, you earn more lives anyway!

Not to mention, those small purchases add up over time (that's why the company that creates Candy Crush Saga is worth 6 billion).

5   Unused Gym memberships. Every January, hoards of people flood their local gym to sign up for memberships, by March, the gyms are almost empty.

Almost every person that has "gym membership" listed in their budget that I've worked with went to the gym less than 4x a month, which means that they could pay per diem and save money. Or better yet, find a way to work out at home like a Fit desk or a Fit2B membership that doesn't require a contract and high monthly rates.

If you're using the gym then it provides value for you, that's great! But unless you've proven to yourself that you can consistently work out for several months, then you're burning money every month. There are quite a few ways to lose weight for lower costs found in this tool and resource guide for weight loss.

6   Lottery. The lottery drives me nuts. We're so focused on getting an unexpected windfall that will solve our financial problems forever that we never even look into what happens when people win the lottery. It's not pretty, guys. In fact, winning the lottery is my biggest fear to date.

When you get a largekely that you'll lose all of it and incur more debt than you can handle.

Basically, if you m amount of money without building the skills needed to manage that large amount of money, it's liake $22,000 a year and have $10,000 in debt, you may feel like you'll never dig yourself out of debt. But that's totally doable (I help people like that every day).

What's terrifying is $400,000 in debt, without the skills necessary to get a job with a high salary. The lottery makes that situation not only possible but likely.

Skip the lottery, and invest in yourself instead. Do you have a hobby that could be turned into a business? Maybe you love photography or writing? Invest in a small business that you can scale up (and skill build) over time.

We did this and turned the blog into a full- time job, while my husband's home brewing hobby has turned into a huge brewery opening in Northern Virginia.

It's still a dollar and a dream, but your odds of winning are much better.

7   Extended warranties. These are almost always a waste of money. This is a good article to explain extended warranties, but the cliff notes version is that extended warranties for electronics, jewelry (engagement rings where you have to get them cleaned every 6 months in order to keep the warranty? Terrible Idea), and cars are all bad ideas.

8   Books. I used to spend a small fortune on books every month. I'm an obsessive reader and am usually reading two books at a time. When we reduced our spending, I stopped buying books completely.

We get every book from the library now. Completely for free.

If my schedule screws up and I end up owing late fees, then I happily pay it considering the amount of money that the library saves me every month.

Switch to the library and pocket the savings. You'll love the extra space in your house, too!

9   Cheap clothes. We love to find a good deal, but with clothing, this means we often have a closet full of cheaply made clothes that don't fit as well. It's a waste of money. The average person uses less than 30% of the clothes in their closet!

Skip the "bargains" and only buy the things that you absolutely love and want to wear every day. Even if you end up buying full-priced clothes, you'll still save a small fortune compared to filling your closet with clothes that don't fit.

10   Timeshares. Repeat after me. Timeshares are never a good idea. Even if you use them all the time. These "prepaid vacation investments" are one of the worst deals you can make and they're extremely hard to get out of.

It boggles my mind to think that we've wasted our hard-earned money on some of these ridiculous purchases in the past. In fact, if you could add up every dollar that you've spent on the items on this list, I bet you could likely pay for a house in cash!

Stay rich.

It's hard to get rich, but it's even harder to stay rich. Your wealth is always going to be affected by the market, and the market has its ups and downs. If you get too comfortable when times are good, you'll quickly drop back to square one when the market hits a slump. If you get a promotion or a raise, or if your ROI goes up a percentage point, don't spend the extra. Save it for when business is slow and your ROI goes down two percentage points.

The terms "rich" and "wealthy" are often used interchangeably, but in fact, they are two different concepts. Wealth relates to how much money you have in the bank, and the security of your assets. To be rich, and stay rich, is more of an attitude, a state of mind that doesn't necessarily relate to your assets, but your quality of life. However, if you're looking to turn a big paycheck or other assets (stocks, real estate, an inheritance, etc.) into lasting wealth, or "stay rich," you'll need to learn to manage your money, making careful choices to ensure your assets won't disappear when the going gets tough. Of course, you can't take your money with you when you die, but you can follow certain steps to stay rich so that it lasts throughout your life.

A.   Organizing Your Finances

1 Diversify your finances in all areas of your life. Diversification is not only the key to building wealth; it's also the key to sustaining the wealth that you have. Ensure that your money is well diversified across a broad spectrum of investment classes including stocks, bonds, mutual funds, real estate, and cash. Different areas of the market will respond differently to the same event, so if you have invested in both stocks and bonds, for instance, your stocks may take a hit in a market

swing, but you may compensate for the loss by a positive movement in the bond market.

Keep in mind that your risk objective may be different than when you were building wealth. You may now find capital preservation (keeping what you have) becoming more important than the risk that comes along with more aggressive (risky) investments.

Understand the risk-return tradeoff. This principle states that the higher the risk you take with an investment, the higher the potential return. Determine your risk tolerance (how much you can safely afford to lose if the investment fails, how much time you have to recover from a potential loss) and talk to your financial adviser about how to balance your investments so that you get some return, but you don't risk financial ruin in the process.

Keep liquidity in mind. Liquidity refers to how quickly and easily an asset or security can be turned into another asset. Cash is extremely liquid, while something like real estate is not. Although you can build a great deal of wealth "on paper" using real estate, you'll also find that it takes time to sell your real estate properties and convert them to cash. If you think you'll ever need cash from your assets in a hurry, it's best not to park too much of that cash into real estate.

Learn more about diversification by reading How to Reduce Financial Risk.

2 Invest in new opportunities. You shouldn't stop trying to build wealth just because you're rich. Some of the richest people in the world are still making investments (check out any episode of Shark Tank for evidence of that). Now that you're rich, it's time to make money work for you instead of you working for money. Find business opportunities that you can invest in to build on the wealth that you have.

Become an angel investor. When you're an angel investor, you'll have the opportunity to invest in startups. You could become a part of the next Uber or Amazon.

This is also a way to "invest with your values" by investing in particular companies you believe in and supporting them in a more direct way.

3 Make your money last. Live on your income, not your liquidation of assets, or keep your spending within what is considered a safe zone. Many experts suggest keeping your spending under 4–6% of your liquid net worth each year.

Avoid liquidating your assets just to buy luxury items; otherwise, you'll be a consumer who loses money and not an investor who earns money. Spending money on things that do not retain value or have no sentimental value is not a good way to make your money last.

4 Develop a budget. Yes, even if you're rich, you're going to need to live on a budget. This is for two reasons.

For starters, a budget is just as important for you if you're rich as it is for someone of lesser means because it's easy to fall victim to the "bottomless pit" mindset. That's when you perceive that you have an infinite supply of money. As a result, you're more likely to burn through it and lose it. If you maintain a budget, you'll be in a better position to preserve your wealth.

A budget is a good idea for everybody. A budget forces you to itemize your spending and practice discipline with your hard-earned wealth.

5 Avoid conspicuous consumption. If you are showing off your wealth by purchasing a variety of luxury goods, it might be a good idea to think about whether you are doing this for genuine reasons or if you are doing so to prove something to others. You are more likely to preserve your wealth and feel fulfilled by not spending it in this way.

6 Set up a trust. If you'd like to preserve your wealth for future generations, consider establishing a financial trust that will prevent spendthrift descendants from squandering away the money that you'd like to pass on to them.

Anthony Fittizzi, managing director and wealth strategist at U.S. Trust, tells his clients that trust places safeguards around how beneficiaries can access and spend the money that's been left to them.

You can also dictate how your money is spent in the future when you set up a trust. That's a great way to ensure that your wealth preservation strategies continue throughout future generations. You may set up a stipulation that the money in the trust can only be used for educational purposes, for instance, or that it will be dispensed in a yearly or monthly sum.

Be aware that once you place your assets in a trust, they are no longer considered to be your assets.

B. Developing the Right Mindset

1 Take your emotions out of wealth preservation. Many people who have wealth suddenly become terrified that they're going to lose it all due to an economic setback or some other unfortunate occurrence. Remember when you evaluate alternative investment options to not get caught up in the hype but to always look at the opportunity from a financial standpoint.

Avoid following the "herd." Just because everybody else is investing in gold or the stock of XYZ Corporation doesn't mean that those are good investments.

When you're evaluating a business deal, look beyond the personality of the person who's proposing the deal and strictly evaluate the merits of the deal on the financials. It's easy to fall in love with a personality, but it won't necessarily make you any money.

Focus on what's important in life. If you're able to spend additional time with your family or give back to the community — doing so may help bring perspective and peace of mind. The old adage that money doesn't buy happiness will be apparent to you when you're wealthy. To truly be rich, you'll want to have friends, family, and a good quality of life, not simply a huge stockpile of assets.

2 Give back to society. Now that you have money, do something good with some of it and you'll find that the laws of the universe work marvelously in your favor. One of the best ways to preserve your wealth is to be generous with the money that you have (and not just because of the tax break!).

There is a reason why rich families have their own foundations (for example, the Rockefeller Foundation). That's because they understand the importance of giving.

CHAPTER NO 2: ENRICHING THROUGH A CAREER

Excel academically

Whether it's a four-year college or vocational training, some successful people pursue further education beyond high school. In the early stages of a career, your employers have little by which to judge you besides your educational background. Higher grades usually lead to higher salaries.

Being a great student doesn't mean hours and hours of studying and having no social life at all! There's always room to improve, so it helps to always check the work you do. This will lead to happiness and satisfaction with not only yourself but what you are doing with your life. And you know: accomplishments are for life; they last! If you get good grades, you're that much closer to a good college, which leads you to a good job. Keep reading to find out how to be more successful in any type of school.

A. General practice

1 Go beyond the surface information. Don't just stop learning at the bare facts. These will not make you any smarter, nor will they give you the analytical tools you need to get straight A's. If you really want to excel in school the most important thing is to always ask why. Learn why things work the way they do, why things matter and then you can apply that knowledge to a vast amount of information and maybe correctly guessing even things you might not have learned about.

2 Use the knowledge of others. This doesn't mean you should cheat - when we say use the knowledge of others, what we mean is that you should talk with friends, family members and teachers about the subjects you are studying. Get their opinions

on topics, see how they would have approached a problem, or learn their method of doing something. In opening your mind to new ways of thinking and doing you should be better prepared to handle almost any academic challenge.

3 Be proactive in your education. Participate in study groups. Get help when you need it. Study over time rather than cramming before a test. Basically, getting straight A's is hard (if it were easy, everyone would do it) so you need to work at it if you want to do this. However, avoid study groups if you tend to talk more than study. Remember, you are only working in a study group to study. Most people tend to forget this when they see a friend, so keep this in mind.

4 Get organized. Consistently keep all assignments or handed back work/handouts separately and in chronological order. Not only does this make life in general easier, but it also helps when exam time comes, especially if there will be a cumulative end-of-year exam. You should also organize your time by allowing yourself plenty of time to study and sleep. Organize your notes and your study space.

Study and do homework in chunks. If you have two days to do a homework assignment, do most of it the first and do the other part the second. Or, if you have a week to learn 10 vocabulary words, learn a few each day and review the words you already learned. This way you'll be less overwhelmed and ultimately have more time free from cramming.

Get a planner. Write down your homework as soon as the teacher assigns it. If a teacher tells you when a project is due or a test will be given write it down. This will help you know what you have to do.

5 Choose the courses you are interested in. If you can, make sure you are studying things you enjoy and can get invested in. You will do better if you care about the material you are studying. This is why you will find that you get the best grades in your favorite classes.

Remember to balance things you enjoy with things you need to know.

6 Be aware of your body clock. The human body learns best at specific times and for some people, it can be in the morning. Be sure you save this time for studying important class material, and leave the rest of the time for less important activities such as socializing. Avoid studying when you are tired. In general, you should try to get at least 8 hours of sleep a night.

7 Give your best effort. You need to have knowledge of each subject you're studying, but it is also important to persevere and go back and revise the subject until you are confident that you will be able to get the right answers during an exam or test. If you don't understand a question on a test then think it through and write it out so that you can see what you are doing.

B. Working Hard in Class

1 Pay attention in class. You can learn so much from just listening so always pay attention in class. Study smart! You should be able to understand the subject better and know what the teacher is talking about prior to a test.

Eat breakfast and if you are prescribed medication or take vitamins make sure you take them before leaving for school. A good breakfast will help keep you awake and focused throughout the day.

2 Ask questions. Ask the teacher relevant questions about the subject. If you do not understand the subject then write down what it is you are having trouble with and ask the teacher if you can have some time to discuss your concerns.

Never be embarrassed to ask questions. Curious students make teachers happy.

3 Read any syllabus you are given and have a general idea about the course subjects and what you may be learning.

For example, if you're in a history class and you're learning about the formation of the United States of America but you see that the next section will be about the American Civil War, think about how those two events could connect to each other.

4 Take notes. **Learn to write down an outline and fill it in with bits and pieces of key information. Write a summary of what you have learned in class to use it for future reference.**

Make notes on what you don't understand so that you are well prepared when your teacher explains those things or you can discuss them with your teacher.

5 Never skip class as you will fall behind and it may affect your grades. **If you are sick and cannot go to school, ask the teacher for any notes on the classes you may have missed. If the teacher is not available for some reason, ask a friend for some information you have missed on the day you were absent.**
6 Talk to your teachers about your grades. **Ask about your quality of work and reasons for any weak grades. Work on any areas of weakness and ask your teacher if your extra work will help improve your grades.**

C. Working Hard At Home

1 Do your homework. **Some college teachers may not always check your homework so it is important to remain motivated. Motivate yourself to do your homework. Homework helps to reinforce what you have learned in class and identify what you don't understand. Study. If you don't have any homework on a subject, read your notes or read any textbooks on the subjects. On average about 10% of your grade is homework but how it is incorporated into your grade really depends on the teacher.**

2 Study a little bit every day at home. This will help cement material in your mind, and you won't have to worry as much if you have a pop quiz or just a teacher who announces tests late.

3 Read ahead in the textbook. This can help you identify areas that you may have more trouble in.

4 Don't procrastinate. Never stay up late doing an assignment unless you have not finished it and it is due very soon. Instead, if you have two weeks to do your assignment, spend the first week outlining and doing the basics. Over the weekend, neatly put it together, and the next week, just put the finishing touches on it, do some editing, and print it out. Don't forget to hand it into your teacher one day before you actually should. This will show your dedication and give your teacher time to suggest revisions.

Starting an assignment ahead of time will also give you time to meet with your teacher and discuss any problems you have, directions you can take, and get other assignment help that is crucial to getting A's. Just going to the extra trouble of asking for help and taking your teacher's advice may earn you a slightly higher grade.

5 Teach the material to someone else. Find a quiet place, maybe in your room, lock the door and imagine you are the teacher explaining the subject to a student. This is also a good way to measure your understanding of the material and explaining it to someone who doesn't understand it at all can often help you develop a better understanding of the material yourself. If you can participate in tutoring programs in school, this serves the same purpose.

6 Get a dedicated study space. Find a space that is only for studying. This may help to minimize distractions and keep you on track. Studying is just another habit and if you teach your brain that a certain desk or room is just for studying then you should have a much easier time focusing and getting work done.

7 Read extra materials if you have time. You can always go on the internet or go to the library and find more books or information about the subjects you are studying. Learning some additional information and adding it into papers or test questions may impress your teachers.

8 Consider getting a tutor if you can afford to. There's nothing wrong with getting in some extra learning and it may make a difference in your grades.

D. Helpful School Tips and Tricks

1 Learn to take great notes. Still, having trouble taking notes that help you later? Try the look, cover, write, and check method, aiding your memory to take in the information you are learning.

2 Learn to outline. Outlining can make any assignment easier by breaking it up into easy to understand chunks. Dealing with these pieces rather than trying to wrap your brain around the whole thing may help you excel.

3 Learn how to spell correctly. If you want to get perfect points on an assignment you're going to need to be sure it's free of spelling and grammar mistakes.

4 Learn how to concentrate.

5 Learn how to do well in school. Doing well in school is about more than just getting A's. Read about how to succeed in school as a whole.

6 Get the subject help. WikiHow offers help in all sorts of subjects, including tutorials in Math, a helping hand in Science, and advice for English. Find more general help in the Education and Communications Category.

Choose the right profession

Look at salary surveys which indicate average annual incomes for specific professions. Your odds of getting rich are diminished if you pursue a career in teaching as opposed to a career in finance. Here are some of the highest-paying jobs in America:

Doctors and surgeons. Anesthesiologists make a whopping $200,000+ per year.

Petroleum engineers. Engineers who work with gas and oil companies can make a very good living. In most cases, they make upwards of $135,000 per year.

Attorneys. Lawyers top out at just above $130,000 per year, making this a lucrative field if you can put in the time.

IT managers and software engineers. If you're good at programming and a whiz at computers, consider this very well-compensated field. IT managers regularly make $125,000 per year.

Choosing the right career can be difficult, but having a defined career direction will help you with getting a job. But with a little hard work, some planning, and some serious self-reflection, you can set yourself on a path towards a fruitful, fulfilling career that can provide for you and your family.

A. Evaluating Your Interests

1 Think about your dream career. There is an old saying that if you're trying to choose a career, you should think about what you would do if you didn't have to work. If you had a million dollars and you could do anything, what would you do? Your answer to that question, while maybe not literally the best

career choice for you, may give you insight into what you should do.

If you want to be a music star, consider going into audio engineering or music composition. These careers are easier to pursue and you will be much more likely to succeed and provide for yourself in the future.

For example, if you want to be an actor, consider going into media broadcasting. You can get a degree in communications or work your way up the chain of command in a local news or other television studios.

For instance, if you want to travel the world, consider becoming an airline steward or stewardess. This is a great way to make a living and pursue your dream of traveling the globe.

If you want to become a CTO, you have to earn a bachelor's degree in a relevant STEM field. It also requires a thorough understanding of all aspects of the business.

2 Assess your hobbies. It is very easy to turn your hobbies or something you love doing into a future career. Many hobbies correspond to real-world needs and positions. Consider what you like to do and how that might fit into a career. Remain humble as you work toward your goal. You may want to work part-time as you get referrals and experience in your desired career.

For example, if you like playing video games, consider becoming a videogame designer, programmer, or QA specialist.

If you like drawing or art, consider becoming a graphic designer.

If you like sports, consider hosting a sports camp or becoming an assistant coach.

3 Consider what you enjoy or enjoyed in school. Academic subjects translate well into future careers but may require more schooling than other types of careers. Your favorite class in high school could very well launch you into your future career but you have to be willing to work for it

> For example, if you loved chemistry, you could look forward to a future career as a lab technician or a pharmacist.

> If you liked English class, consider becoming an editor or a copywriter.

> If you enjoyed math, consider becoming an actuary or an accountant.

B. Assessing Your Skills

1 Think about what you are or were good at in school. Think about the subjects you excelled in school. Though it may not be your favorite thing to do, choosing a career based on something you are skilled at can help you excel and provide yourself a secure future.

> Look at the examples from the previous step if you need ideas.

2 Consider what skills you excel in. If you are particularly good at certain skills, such as fixing things or making things, this can provide you with a great future career. Schooling may or may not be necessary, but skilled labor is often in demand and you will find it fairly easy to find work.

> For example, carpentry, auto repair, construction, and electrical work all benefit from people who are good at fixing things or working with their hands. These also tend to be stable, well-paying jobs.

> Other skills, such as a skill for cooking, can also be easily turned into a career.

3 Assess your interpersonal skills. If your skills lie more in helping and communicating with other people, there are jobs for you as well. People who communicate and interact with others well can easily get careers as social workers or in marketing and similar business positions.

If you're more the type to take care of others, consider nursing or work as an administrative assistant or office manager.

4 Ask someone if you don't know. Sometimes it's hard for us to see the areas in life where we excel. If you don't think you're good at anything, ask your parents, other family members, friends, or teachers what they think you'd be good at. Their ideas might surprise you!

Your friends and family can also help you network and get you in touch with people in your chosen field. You can also join a Meetup to meet others that are involved with the work you hope to do.

C. Considering Your Current State

1 Explore yourself. Figuring out what you should do with your life may sometimes require you to get to know yourself better. If you want a career that will really make you happy, you have to have a very good understanding of what you want and what you enjoy. For some people, this means taking some time off to decide what's important to them.

There is nothing wrong with this, so don't feel bad. It's more important that you figure your life out as early as possible, rather than getting knee-deep in a career which makes you hate your life.

2 Consider your financial situation. Your ability to pursue or change careers may hinge on your financial situation. Some career paths require special schooling and this is sometimes expensive. However, you should not feel that being poor restricts you from getting the education you want.

There are lots of government programs to help you pay for schools, as well as scholarships, grants, and apprenticeship programs.

3 Think about the education you will have as you enter a career. It is important to consider what education you already have or will have as you begin pursuing a career. If finances may prevent you from pursuing more schooling, you may need to consider what you already have. It may also be necessary to stick with your existing high school or college degree if there are time limitations or other restrictions.

If you find that you are limited to jobs relating to the degree you already have, consult with a career counselor to find out what options are available to you.

4 Determine if you want to go to school. If restrictions do not bar you from pursuing more schooling, you may want to consider this option. Not everybody excels in school or needs a traditional college education, but most career paths have associated training which you can do and will help you advance more quickly.

Technical colleges, for example, maybe a good option for those who would prefer not to pursue a traditional education.

5 Do more research. If you're still confused, consider doing more research on this topic. You can find more helpful information here or consult with your adviser or college of choice.

D. Contemplating Your Future

1 Consider the careers you have easy access to. **Consider what career options are available for you to easily move into. These would be careers in which you have both the necessary skills and an "in."**

Examples would be working for the same company as one of your parents, working for a family business, or working for a friend. If your options are limited, choosing a career in which you can quickly enter maybe your best option.

2 Examine your future financial security. **One of the most important things to consider is if the career path you're choosing will provide you with an acceptable level of financial security. In other words, will you be able to make enough money to support yourself and your family?**

Do the math to figure out what your take-home salary needs to be. Take into account your health insurance and retirement options as well. You may want to see a financial advisor before making any decisions.

Remember, this doesn't have to be a lot of money or enough money by somebody else's standards. All that matters is that it's enough for you and what you want for your life.

3 Scrutinize your future job stability. **Job markets fluctuate as society needs different things at different times. Certain jobs are also always in demand or frequently unstable. You will need to consider if the career you choose is stable enough for you and your desires for the future.**

For example, many people recently went into law school and racked up often in excess of $100,000 in school debt because they thought they'd be making a very high wage in the future. However, law positions are not in demand as much the last few years and now those people have huge debts and no way to pay them.

Another example is working as a writer or any career based on freelance work. You may sometimes have plenty of work but there may be years when you have almost nothing. Working in this way requires a certain level of determination and discipline and is not for everybody.

4 Look at the Occupational Outlook Handbook. **One way for you to gauge if a career option is a good idea is to look it up in the Occupational Outlook Handbook. This is a guide, compiled by the Bureau of Labor Statistics, which looks at what kind of education is required for different jobs, how much people in those careers make on average, and how much the demand for that job is likely to increase or decrease.**

5 Make a dream board. **A dream board is a wonderful tool for organizing your aspirations. It can also help you hold yourself accountable as you work toward reaching your goals. Find pictures online or in magazines and paste them onto poster boards. Choose inspiring quotes and add trinkets as well, if desired.**

Choose the right location

Go where the good jobs are. If you want to pursue finance, for example, there are far greater opportunities in big cities than in rural, low-populated areas. If you want to build a startup, you'll probably want to consider going to Silicon Valley. If you want to make it big in the entertainment industry, go to LA or New York City.

Deciding where to live is a big decision. Do not make it lightly – but also remember that your choice does not need to be final. Take some time to think about what's most important to you. Weigh your ideals against your realities. When the time comes: make the choice that feels the most right and take the leap!

A. Exploring Your Options

1 Make a list. Write down the cities, states, nations, or regions that float to the top of your mind when you think about where you might want to live. Your list may be very short or very long. If you don't already have a few places in mind, then you will need to do more research in order to better understand what you're looking for.

2 Research. Run a web search, talk to people, and read guidebooks in order to learn more about each place that finds its way onto your list. Read about the history, the culture, the scenery, the economy. Try to pin down what it is, exactly, that draws you to this place.

Ask your friends. If you are considering moving to a city, and you know someone who has lived in that city before: be sure to ask this person for their perspective. Keep in mind that what works for one person does not always work for another!

3 Notice the trends. Look for the common factors between the places that you are considering living. Then, use these patterns to help yourself understand what sort of place, generally, you are looking for: urban, rural, or suburban; mountainous or seaside; east coast or west coast. Once you've identified a few similar options, try to parse out the more subtle differences between these places.

If you listed San Francisco, Portland, and Seattle, consider that these are all relatively young, affluent, tech-driven cities along the West Coast of the United States. Perhaps you are looking for a certain sort of energy that you identify with these particular urban centers. To narrow down your decision, examine the differences between these cities.

If you listed Montana, Alaska, and Colorado, then you probably want to live somewhere mountainous, outdoorsy, and relatively unpopulated. There are many similarities between these three states, but there are also many differences. Research each state to better understand the difference.

4 Visit. If you are intrigued by the idea of a place, try to check it out in person before you make any serious decisions. Take any opportunity that you get to visit the area, speak with the people, and imagine yourself living there. Try staying there on holiday if you can, renting temporary accommodation to get a real feel of living in your desired location.

If you are thinking of moving relatively nearby, then you can visit on a weekend or a day off. If you are thinking of living somewhere far away, then make sure that you have the time and resources to get there and back.

B. Evaluating Aesthetics

1 Consider the culture. Learn about the music scene, the party scene, the food scene – anything that you think would enhance your quality of life. Try to grasp the cultural idiosyncrasies that make each place unique. Read about the ratio of younger people to older people, and try to see the trends in why people are moving to a particular place.

Perhaps your favorite band or a beloved author hails from a certain city. Maybe you've heard that a city has a notoriously active and outdoorsy populace.

Living around others who are in the same socioeconomic bracket can be more comfortable than living among people who make considerably more or less than yourself. Whether you will be renting or owning a home in your new area, try consulting with a real estate agent to get a better idea of the neighborhood.

2 See the romance in a place. It is important to make an informed and practical decision, but you should also find a reason to be enthused about the place you're going to live. Create a mental image of what life would be like here, and then evaluate whether that life is something you want.

3 Understand what the climate is like. Determine whether you want to live somewhere hot, cold, wet, dry – near the coast or in the mountains. Basic research on a city or region should give you a good idea of the weather patterns. Consider the effects that a different climate (say, a very rainy place, or somewhere that freezes over in the winter) will have upon your lifestyle and your goals. Consider the temperature, the average precipitation, the air pollution, and the seasonal flux.

Some people suffer from Seasonal Affective Disorder (SAD), which is a cyclical depression pattern related to the changing of the seasons. People often find themselves most down in the winter or the rainy season, when the skies are cold and overcast.

If you are unsure of the climate in a particular area, the National Oceanic and Atmospheric Administration (NOAA) have excellent data on everything from temperature to air pollution.

4 Learn about the risk of natural disasters. This can also help swing your decision, although it may not be the weightiest concern. Some areas face a high risk of hurricanes and tornadoes, while other areas get a lot of earthquakes. Some areas are prone to drought and others to mighty storms. Inform yourself of the danger so that you can make a conscious choice.

C. Getting Practical

1 Take money into account. Move to a place that you can afford, but that also provides you with the opportunities you want. Your money will go much further in some regions than it will in others. On the other hand, the jobs that you'll find in a more expensive area will also typically pay you more. This is the dilemma: the places with the most opportunity are often the most expensive to live, and the most affordable places are often less conducive to building a career.

Do not let money be the only deciding factor. Yes, you should move to a place where you'll be able to support yourself and your family. First and foremost, however, you should be excited about where you're going.

2 Think about work. Factor your current and future career into the equation. Consider searching for jobs in potential new cities just to get an idea for what's out there. Look for areas that feature a lot of jobs in a field that interests you.

If you plan to keep your current job, then it may not be feasible to move somewhere that involves a lengthy commute.

3 Make the right choice for your children. If you will be moving with children or expecting children, then research which areas have the best opportunities for education. Imagine how the culture and opportunities of a given area will impact the way that a child is raised. Pick a place that will provide a nurturing and stimulating environment for your children to call "home."

Think about the sort of support system that will be available. It can be much easier to raise children, both financially and logistically, if you are living near a network of family and close friends.

If you homeschool your child, make sure to look into homeschooling groups for a given area. Some regions are much friendlier to homeschoolers then others.

Get entry-level job and work up

Working your way up a company tends to be an effective way to become familiar with various facets of a company. Mastering a number of tasks and positions and getting recognized for your competence can be reaffirming of your value to the company. Climbing the corporate ladder requires goal definition, commitment, responsibility, and productivity. With a positive attitude and strong work ethic, you should be on your way to the top in no time!

Play the numbers game. Apply to many places and subject yourself to lots of interviews. When you get your job, stick with it, and get the experience you need to advance.

A. Planning Goals for the Future

1 Define your corporate goal. Your ultimate goal may be to hold a top leadership position in a company or to manage a large department. Be specific about your career goals. Write your goals down and keep them on your desk so that you can remind yourself to stay motivated.

2 Ask veteran employees about their experiences. Ask them to explain to you how they worked their way up the corporate ladder. Their advancement paths and strategies might resonate with you and give you inspiration. However, remember that each person's path to success is unique.

Approach your co-worker when they have free time. Tell them that you admire their work and that you hope to increase your value to the company. Ask them: "How do you recommend pursuing a promotion here?" or "How did you work your way to your current position?" You could even praise them for a specific task that they recently completed, and ask them how they went about accomplishing it.

3 Remain motivated in your position. Understanding your role's value to the overall process and the company will allow you to demonstrate the proper commitment. Maintain a positive attitude; you never know who is paying attention.

4 Understand the company structure. There may be multiple departments with various levels of management within each. Familiarize yourself with the company structure by studying its organizational chart and learning the important players in management.

B. Making Yourself Invaluable

1 Demonstrate your commitment. Show the higher-ups that your goals align with the goals of the company. Stuffing envelopes or filing paperwork may seem below your skill level, but remind yourself that your work is important and may lead to company sales. Bringing an executive their morning coffee may seem far removed from your goal of being an executive, but it will allow you to build interpersonal relationships and will help the executive to better perform daily tasks.

2 Network with co-workers. Build positive relationships with people at all levels of the company. One of your co-workers may become your boss someday. A colleague with whom you have a personality clash may wind up in a position to chime in about your suitability for a promotion. Treat everyone with respect and fairness, and they will be likely to pay you respect in return.

Show your appreciation for others. Acknowledge the contributions of colleagues who help you solve difficult problems. When leading others, let them know that you appreciate their individual strengths.

Greet people warmly. Whether in an elevator with a top executive or standing in the company cafeteria line with an employee from another department, take the opportunity to introduce yourself and strike up a conversation.

3 Attend company-wide social functions. It might be tempting to skip the company's holiday event, but attending such social gatherings will allow you to interact with a wide variety of company employees. It will also increase your visibility and your chances of being viewed as an integral member of the company.

4 Take on additional responsibilities. Lighten your boss' workload by offering to oversee a small project. Stay late to master new software, make sales calls, or organize paperwork. Make sure that the additional tasks that you pursue contribute to greater productivity without jeopardizing your relationships with colleagues.

Avoid stepping on other people's toes or crossing boundaries. Your goal is not to outdo your supervisor or to highlight the inadequacy of your colleagues, but rather to offer vital support.

C. Broadening Your Skill Set

1 Enroll in classes to strengthen skills. Learn the information and skills that you need to progress to the next level in the company. If your goal is to work your way up from administrative assistant to project coordinator to project manager to department director, always prepare for the next job in the sequence of promotions.

Look for courses offered online, or skim your local newspaper for opportunities. Community college courses can also be a helpful and affordable option. Ask your co-workers or your boss if they have any recommendations for you.

2 Take courses offered by the company. Some companies offer training and development programs to help employees gain new skills. When given a choice, use these opportunities wisely by choosing classes that will prepare you for a future role. Your boss will be impressed that you are working to better yourself in order to become more of an asset to the company.

3 Learn a new language. **Many companies will be more apt to promote someone who is knowledgeable in more than one language since it gives them an edge over their competition and helps them to get their message across to a larger audience of consumers.**

Find out whether your company has an office or market in a foreign country. You will have a better chance at career advancement if you learn the language in that particular country. If your company has an office in Berlin, for instance, it could help you to learn German. Or if your company does business in Madrid, you may want to become fluent in Spanish.

D. Advancing Your Career

1 Apply to relevant job openings. **Many companies tend to promote from within, since they value employees who wish to stay with their company for a long time. Ask your employer if there is an internal job postings site, as some opportunities might be shared within the company before they decide to outsource or open the role to new hires.**

Be sure that you possess the right qualifications and experience for any position to which you apply. Be realistic about your capabilities, and make logical progressions.

2 Ask for a promotion. **If you have been working hard in your position for over a year, and feel that you are qualified for a higher position, it cannot hurt to inquire about an opportunity for promotion. Apply for the job before approaching your boss. Be honest about your goals, and about why you think you would be a good fit for the new role.**

Discussing a salary raise or the terms of your employment with your boss can be intimidating. Describe how you have positively contributed to the company thus far, and how you hope to assist the company in achieving its goals going forward. Create a presentation highlighting your skills and your job performance. Say, "I am the best candidate for the role because..." and then list your assets.

Have confidence in yourself, and remain open to the possibility that your boss may not be quite ready to promote you. Do not give up; instead, use this as motivation to work even harder so that your employer will realize your full potential.

3 Be patient. Plan to stay in each position for a reasonable amount of time. Although the right amount of time is largely dependent on the needs of the particular company, staying in a position for at least 1 year is a common expectation. It often takes that long to master the responsibilities, to contribute value to your company, and to train others before being promoted.

Change jobs and employers

Once you've gotten some experience under your belt, consider finding a new job. By changing your environment, you can increase your pay and experience different corporate cultures. Don't be afraid to do this several times. If you're a valued employee, it's also likely your current company may offer you a raise or other benefits if they know you're looking at leaving.

How happy can you be if your job makes you miserable? Millions of people go to work every day dreading the next 8 hours. This doesn't have to be you! Believe it or not, it's possible to enjoy your job and to get paid for it.

A. Starting the Transition

1 Try to stay at your current job while beginning the search for a new job. The search for a new job can take quite a while — by some measures, one month for each $10k in expected salary. If you're looking for a well-paying job, that's a lot of time to be out of work. If your job is truly horrendous and you can't take it anymore, consider quitting. Otherwise, try to stick it out. Your wallet will thank you, as will your future employer: It's easier to get a job if you already have a job, as you're considered "employable."

2 Make sure the grass isn't dead. You know the saying: "The grass is always greener on the other side." A lot of people dislike their jobs for good reason, but some believe the grass is always greener on the other side, and get a rude awakening when they switch jobs, only to find their situation worse on the other side.

It's extremely tough to gauge whether your future job could be worse than your current one. The fact that you want to switch jobs should tip you off that you're unhappy; just make sure you're unhappy for good reason, not some unrealistic expectation of what the work world is like.

3 Start thinking about what kind of job you'd like to switch to. Are you merely switching jobs within the same sector, or are you switching careers? There's a pretty big difference. Switching jobs in the same industry doesn't require nearly as much planning and legwork as switching careers.

Imagine what you'd do if you had all the money in the world. What would you spend your time doing? Would you spend your time traveling and writing about the experience? Would you spend your days cooking? A lot of our most enjoyable pursuits don't pay as well as the "lucrative" ones, but if you're truly good at what you love to do, you probably stand to make a good deal of money *and* have fun doing it at the same time.

Recall your most enjoyable accomplishments and experiences, especially those that are deeply felt and emotionally fulfilling. What are you good at doing? Many people find that they enjoy doing the things they're naturally good at.

4 Start keeping a career journal or diary. It may sound cheesy, but a journal is a pursuit that will force you to collect your thoughts and start to be honest about your feelings and aspirations (which is a tough thing to do). Use your journal to collect all your positive thoughts, insights, and leads that you gather over the course of your job search.

5 Stoke your natural curiosity. Get curious. There are several reasons why it pays to be curious. For one, the curious person is usually a learning person, and employers are looking for candidates who are *eager*, not just willing, to learn on the job. Second, the curious person is more likely to find a better job fit for him- or herself by asking "why?"

Ask yourself *why* you like what you do. Begin to probe. Perhaps you're passionate about sprinting, for example, but don't excel at it. If you tried to become a sprinter, you probably wouldn't succeed. But if you realized that you loved the physiology behind sprinting, you might choose to become a sports doctor. The curious person constantly tries to understand more about both the world and themselves, making the job/career switch easier.

6 Decide whether to tell your boss that you'll be looking for a new job. This is one of those really tough decisions that crops up as you switch jobs. There are advantages and disadvantages to telling your boss. Ultimately, it'll be up to you to make an informed decision about what's best to do in your case:

Advantages: You could get a counter-offer to stay which would make your job more bearable, although not necessarily more meaningful; you give your boss ample time to find a replacement; you leave your current company not having burned bridges and having been honest about your feelings.

Disadvantages: You could not get a job offer for several months, leaving you in a "transitional" period permanently; your boss may think you're simply angling for a pay bump; your boss may begin to distrust your work and make you feel less relevant as time goes on.

B. Pounding the Pavement

1 Sort out all the personal documents you need to start applying to different jobs. Get all the administrivia out of the way pretty early on. Touch up your resume or spruce up your CV. Bone up on how to write a cover letter if you need to. Begin diplomatically soliciting letters of recommendation from people who know you well and are positively disposed to saying something nice about you. Other things to think about:

Learn   how   to interview   well and   form excellent interview questions

Learn how to protect your online reputation

Sort out your elevator pitch if you haven't already

2 Start networking. Networking is probably the single most important step in your new job search. That's because referrals and personal connections (and, let's face it, nepotism) make up the bulk of how people land jobs these days. Why? Referred candidates tend to perform better than random hires and stay on the job longer.[2] So the next time you drag yourself to a networking event when you know you could be sitting at home in your PJs eating ice cream, tell yourself it's for your new, unrealized job.

Remember that people hire people, not resumes. Making an impression in a face to face human exchange is extremely important. People hire people that they like, not necessarily those with the best resume or even qualifications.

Networking can seem pretty daunting, especially for introverts. The most important things to remember are that the other person is probably nervous, too, and that no one thinks about you as much as you think about yourself. If you mess up, no biggie; just brush it off! They're probably thinking about themselves, not about you.

3 Identify and speak to people who do what you think you'd like to do. Say you want to switch jobs and become a parole officer, for example. Well, try to find someone (a friend of a friend will do) who's a parole officer and ask them out to lunch for an informational interview. It might even be a good idea to talk to a warden and ask them the qualities of a good parole officer, for example. More often than you might guess, informational interviews lead directly or indirectly to job offers.

During your informational interview, ask them questions about their personal career path and their current job:

How did you find the job?

What did you do before you were a [occupation]?

What's the most satisfying part of your job? The least?

What's a typical day look like for you?

What's your advice for someone trying to break into the field?

4 Establish personal relationships with companies or organizations you determine you'd like to work for. It's not called "pounding the pavement" for nothing. Going into companies in person and asking to speak to HR about job openings isn't as high success as networking or getting a referral, but it's higher success than blindly stabbing in the dark with online applications. Here's what you do:

Reach out to HR directly and describe your experience or your desired job. Market yourself -- — briefly. Then ask: "Are there any positions open that might align with my skills and expertise?" Prepare to leave your contact info and/or a resume or CV with the HR department.

Don't be discouraged if HR effectively says no. Ask if you can be updated if/when a position comes up and leave your contact info. If you're still interested in the organization after a month or two, follow up with HR and show renewed interest. Not a lot of people do this, and it shows real courage and persistence — two great traits to have.

5 Apply to different jobs online. Applying to different jobs online via job bulletins is impersonal and easy, which explains why so many people do it. It's fine if you apply to jobs online, but you should probably couple your online search with more personal interactions to up your chances of success. The goal is to distinguish yourself from the herd, not blend in!

6 Volunteer, if necessary, to try out a job or career for size. If you're not finding much luck searching for leads, volunteer in your free time for a position you care about. It doesn't have to be long hours, but it should be something that exposes you to the real meat of the job. Volunteering looks great on resumes and occasionally turns into a paid position.

C. Finalizing the Transition

1 Practice job interviewing before the real deal. You can practice with a friend or mentor, or simply try to secure as many interviews as possible and learn as you go. Getting a few practice interviews is really good practice; you'll be surprised how good the mileage is when it comes time to ace your interview.

2 Ace the interview. Whether it's a group interview, phone interview, behavioral interview, or something in between, interviews can be daunting because we're asked to distill our personalities and skills into bite-size sound bites while appearing relaxed and personable all the while. Few things in life can seem as difficult as your first job interview. Here are a couple of pointers to remember as you get ready to jump into the world of interviewing again:

Just like networking, the person interviewing you is probably nervous as well. They want to make a good impression, too. They want you to think favorably of their company. The stakes might not be as high for them, but don't for a second think that being in the driver's seat for an interview is a piece of cake. Part of their performance is going to be judged on the merit of the candidates that they bring in.

Pay attention to your body language during the interview. If you get an interview, it means there's something about you that the potential employer thinks might fit in their system. That's great. And while you can't change your skills and your expertise mid-stride in the interview, you can change how you present yourself. Look the interviewer in the eye; remember to smile; work on your handshake; be polite and err on the side of modesty without being totally abnegating.

Keep your interview answers succinct. When you're under the heat of the microscope, time starts to dilate, and a lot of people feel like they're not talking enough when in fact they're talking too much. Pause after you feel like you've incisively addressed the question. If the interviewer maintains eye contact without speaking, that's probably a cue that they expect further elaboration; if the interviewer launches into the next question, you've kept your answer at a good length.

Keep a positive attitude during and after the interview. There will be interviews that you bomb that's just a fact of life. Don't get down on yourself for a poor interview. Instead, learn from your mistakes and apply those lessons to future interviews. During the interview, especially, don't let negativity affect your approach. Many people think they do much worse than they come off.

3 Follow up with all the interviewers — job and information — you sit down with. Show continued interest in the people you've talked with. After your interview, shoot off a quick email saying how pleasant it was to meet the person. If you didn't clarify how long you were expected to wait during the interview, clarify now.

People respond to other people, not necessarily to paper. Making sure you treat the interviewer like a person, first and foremost, will go a long way toward cementing your eligibility as a top candidate.

4 When you get your job offer, negotiate a salary and benefits. A lot of applicants are a little meek when it comes to negotiating their salary because they're just happy they have jobs. Believe in your self-worth, and translate that faith to your financial worth. Research the starting salaries of similarly-experienced candidates in similar fields and geographic regions. Then, when it comes to naming a number, name a specific figure like $62,925 instead of merely saying $60k — it will make you appear like you've really done your homework.

5 Don't submit your letter of resignation until you've landed a job you know you're going to take. Wait until you've got an offer in writing before you go to your current — soon to be ex-boss and let him or her know that you'll be leaving. Try to schedule the start of your new job so that you give your old company at least two weeks to find a replacement. Any less time and your old company will be manically struggling to find a replacement, making them feel resentful towards you. Any more time and you'll begin to feel like a lost ducky who's overstaying their welcome and becoming increasingly irrelevant.

6 Transition from one job to the next without burning any bridges. It's hard to stay focused or mask your enmity for some employees when you know you're going to leave soon. Dig in. Here are some things that you should remember while you're waiting out your final two weeks at your old job:

Don't pack your bags before you've left. Don't check out. Stay focused during your last days on the job. Instill trust in your manager that you're fully present and committed to doing your work for as long as you stay at the company.

Don't speak out publicly against any of your old bosses or colleagues. This kind of public guillotining gets around and doesn't exactly keep relations tight with your old employer or reassure your new one.

Say goodbye to your old colleagues. Shoot out an email blast to everyone (if you're leaving a small company) or those people you've worked with (if it's a larger company) letting them know you're moving on. Keep it quick and simple — no need to elaborate on why. Then write personal notes to select individuals you established a really good working relationship with. Let them know how grateful you are to have worked with them.

7 Settle into your new job! When it's time, change jobs or careers until you find the right one, the best one, the inevitable one, the one that engages you in "work that's a worthy expression of who you are." Then make it your own.

CHAPTER NO 3: REDUCING LIVING EXPENSES
Try extreme couponing.

It's one of the best feelings in the world when you can get paid to take home stuff you regularly use. If you do this right, you can actually *get paid a coupon*. At worst, you'll save a few extra bucks that you can tuck away for a rainy day. At best, you'll get tons of free stuff and will be richer in the process.

Everyone wishes that they could shop for their favorite items and earn money instead of giving it away. Well, extreme coupons claim to be able to do just that. With a little time and organization, you will be on your way to slashing your costs and even earning money back. This article tells you how to find coupons, use Catalina's and get extreme with your savings.

A. Finding Coupons

1 Get a cheap Sunday newspaper subscription. Subscribe to a statewide paper and a paper from your town or a nearby town as long as the money you save from the coupons that you find pays for your subscription.

Find coupons in the inserts from companies like Smart Source. You can usually find 2 to 3 dedicated coupons inserts every Sunday.

Check for sale fliers from your favorite stores. These may have coupons printed across the bottom of the page or next to some of your favorite items.

Find out when your favorite store prints its sales flyer. If your favorite grocery store prints its flier in Thursday's paper, then consider subscribing on Thursday as well.

2 Sign up for store emails. Many stores will email coupons to you or send you an electronic copy of their sales fliers. If you purchase or sign up for a loyalty card from a company, be sure that you provide your email address and indicate that you want to receive messages containing deals.

3 Look for coupons on reputable websites. Some ideas include:

SmartSource.com

Coupons.com

Redplum.com

CouponNetwork.com

Groupon.com

4 Subscribe to a coupon clipper website, such as New England coupon clippers. These subscriptions will deliver coupons to your mailbox based on deals available in your region.

5 Check the websites or Facebook pages of your favorite companies. If your favorite companies have a Twitter feed, then subscribe so you can get a link to deals.

6 Clip coupons from your favorite magazines. All you, for instance, is a magazine sold by Walmart that is chock full of great coupons.

7 Be observant when you walk around stores. You may find coupons on store shelves next to your favorite products. You can also look at the front of your store for a machine that dispenses deals. Some stores have machines into which you can insert your loyalty card and receive coupons based on your past purchase patterns.

8 Seek out QR codes. You can scan these codes with your mobile phone and be led to an online coupon that you can use at checkout. A QR code looks something like this:

Purchase a mobile phone app that will read QR codes, such as QR Reader for iPhone or QR Droid for Android. Tap on the app to open it.

Generally, you point your camera at the code and press the key in the bottom center of your phone to activate a scanner. You then scan the code and the coupon or website opens on your phone. Different apps have different instructions, so check your app to be sure.

9 Organize a coupon swap. If you have friends who also love extreme coupons, then get together and swap coupons that you don't use for some that are more valuable to you.

B. Learning to Love Catalina's (In-Store Coupons Generated at the Cash Register)

1 Collect Catalina's after every transaction. Note the expiration date on each. They usually have to be used within 10 days to 3 months of the day they print out.

2 Register on a website like Coupon Network. You can list the stores at which you most commonly shop and receive information about Catalina's that they are currently printing.

3 Check forum comments on sites like Hot Coupon World, Slick Deals, or Pinching Your Pennies. Extreme couponers leave comments in the forum letting you know what deals are currently out there in the form of Catalina's.

4 Roll your Catalina's. For instance, if you receive a Catalina for $1 off 3 jars of applesauce, try this trick:

Come back into the store and buy more applesauce. Use the Catalina at the cash register. If you're lucky, another Catalina will be given to you after your transaction.

Go back for more applesauce as long as the Catalinas keep printing. You can usually get away with a maximum of 3 transactions per store

5 Go to multiple locations of your favorite store. For instance, if you know that your grocery store has 4 locations close to your home, then visit all 4 locations. Use the Catalina's to stock up on your favorite items. Be aware that not every location will print the same Catalina's, but if the stores are close-by, it's worth exploring.

6 Stack your Catalina's. If you receive in-store coupons for $5 off a $30 purchase, then save the Catalina's for when you need to purchase expensive items, like meat or seafood. Then, use as many as you can in 1 transaction to save money on these items.

7 Bring your Catalina's to a competitor. If a store is willing to accept competitor coupons, then you can get the same deals in a different store instead of waiting on your preferred store to run a sale.

8 Share the wealth. Go to a coupon forum yourself and let your fellow extreme couponers know what Catalinas you found. If you are generous with your tips, then your fellow couponers will reciprocate.

C. You Have Coupons, Now Use Them

1 Wait for a good sale. One good idea is to use a website like The Grocery Game. This site will list the sales flyers for your favorite stores. When you see an item in the flyer, and you know you have a coupon for that item, then it's time to save yourself some money. Otherwise, you can do the research yourself.

2 Organize your coupons. Try 1 of these methods:

Use baseball card holders inside a 3-ring binder to make your coupons easy to reach. Then, use divider tabs to split your coupons into sections by product, by store or by another method that makes sense to you.

Use an alphabetically organized accordion file. Place your coupons in order by product name. Sort through each pocket weekly and put soon-to-expire coupons at the front of the pocket so you don't forget to use them.

If you can't be bothered cutting out the coupons to insert into separate card slots in a binder, simply hole punch the page and attach a pair of small scissors (such as a child's safety pair) by a string to the binder. That way, you can cut out the coupon as you find the product.

3 Write or print out a list of your current coupons. You can do this on an Excel spreadsheet.

As you walk around, you can place the relevant coupon into a small envelope sitting in your bag or in the cart, in readiness to hand over all coupons for items you found to the cashier.

As you use coupons, mark them off your list with a pen or pencil. When you get home, delete them from your spreadsheet.

4 Purchase multiple items. If your store is selling cereal in a "Buy 2, Get the 3rd Free" promotion, and you have a coupon for the same cereal, then get as much cereal as you can under the terms of the deal.

Watch the language on the sale flyer to make sure the store has a reasonable limit on the amount of items that you can buy under the promotion.

Avoid buying perishable items in bulk. For example, don't stockpile dairy or produce.

At home, shop from your stash. If you don't know what to cook for dinner, then choose an item from your bulk purchases to avoid ordering takeout or running to the store for something you can live without.

5 Stack your coupons. If you have manufacturer's coupons and store coupons, then combine them to get even more money off your purchase.

6 Order items that are sold out. If your store will let you place a bulk order for the items listed on your coupon, then don't be afraid to ask.

7 Go during off-peak hours. Extreme coupon transactions take time, and other customers will feel impatient if you hold up the line with your coupons. Also, cashiers can become frustrated with many coupons because of not only transaction length but also confusion about store policies. You need to go at a time the store isn't too busy to minimize conflict.

8 Leave your kids at home. Extreme coupon transactions require clear communication. If your children are running wild or trying to talk to you while you're interacting with the cashier, then you won't be able to concentrate on what you're doing. Find a babysitter for your early extreme coupon adventures.

9 Be open to various brands. You may have to go with a brand that isn't your tried and true choice to get a deal. As long as the difference in taste and quality is negligible, the savings will be worth it.

10 Know the store's policy and have a copy of it with you. This is simply a safeguard against cashiers who aren't aware of store policies themselves and don't really want to have to deal with your extreme coupling.

It is far easier to say "we don't accept that" than to go to the effort of ringing it all through, so be prepared to politely but firmly clarify the appropriateness of your coupon actions by pointing out the store policy.

You will often find the policy online; if not, ask the store manager for a copy.

11 Use appropriate coupon etiquette. Stick to these good practices:

Be considerate to your cashier and to the people lined up behind you.

Never photocopy coupons. Some stores will no longer accept coupons that even appear to be photocopied.

Avoid hoarding. Items usually go on sale on a 6 to 8 week cycle. Stock up on enough to take you through the sales cycle and no more. Don't become a person who stacks cases of toothpaste under your bed.

Don't commit fraud. Avoid using coupons for items other than the item printed on the paper. Also, never alter existing coupons or print off counterfeits.

D. Other Money Saving Practices

1 Know if your store price matches. Some stores will match and even undercut the price of the same product sold in other stores. Just bring in a sales flyer from the competing store as proof of the price.

2 Plan your menus around store sales and your coupon inventory. You might feel limited at first, but you'll come to enjoy the creative challenge of coming up with meals that your family will enjoy at a low cost.

3 Shop at stores that offer discounts on fuel. If you can accumulate points toward a fuel purchase by shopping at a

certain store, then you'll save money on top of your coupon discounts.

4 Know when items go on clearance. For instance, buy a winter coat in the spring, or purchase bedding and home items in January. Look for big post-holiday clearance sales or summer clearance sales.

5 Take advantage of credit card rewards. Don't go crazy with your credit card just to get bargains, but use it wisely to help yourself save money. Some cards offer gift cards to use in certain stores or discounts on certain products. You can also earn rewards toward restaurants, airline tickets, or hotel stays.

6 Compare prices of brand-name items to generic items. Sometimes, a store's generic product is cheaper even than a brand-name product combined with a coupon offer. The generic version is often comparably good, so be open-minded.

7 Donate some bulk items to charity. If you can't possibly use all those boxes of pancake mix, then donate them to needy families in your community.

8 Have realistic expectations. You're probably going to have to coupon for at least 3 months to build your stockpile of goods. Then, you will begin to see significant savings.

Buy in bulk

It's not the easiest way to shop, but it's usually the most efficient. If you can borrow or buy into a membership to a bulk retailer like Costco, it can make real financial sense. In some cases, you can find brand-name products for sale at serious discounts.

If you're hungry and you like chicken, buy four pre-cooked Chickens at Costco at the end of the day, when they go on sale. Sometimes they'll drop from $5 each to $2.50 each, meaning that you get at least ten hearty meals for about $1 each! Freeze any chickens that you don't eat immediately.

Whether you are moving to a new home or just want to save some cash, understanding how to buy in bulk can save you a ton of money. Contrary to popular belief, buying in bulk is more than just stocking up on toilet paper. While it might be exciting to buy 20 rolls at once at a seemingly unbeatable price, you want to be sure you are actually saving money, and that your new home can handle the bulk items you buy. Moving is a great time to build up your necessities and stock up. Use this guide to figure out how to buy in bulk for your new home, ensuring that you save money as you go.

A. What it means to buy in Bulk

Buying in bulk means that you buy large quantities of one product at one time. For example, you can purchase 10 boxes of batteries at once, and often for a fraction of their individual sale price.

It might seem as though the goal of buying in bulk is just to get as much as possible for as little as possible, but the truth is that when you buy in bulk your primary goal should be to minimize your cost per unit. That way you can easily compare prices between different brands and retailers.

Each unit is a portion of an item that can be measured by the pound, gram, ounce, and so on. Paper goods such as paper towels are often priced per square foot and liquids are generally priced by the ounce. Let's take shampoo as an example. One unit is measured as one ounce of shampoo, not one bottle, so if you bought multiple bottles of shampoo in bulk, you would calculate the price per unit by the total number of ounces you bought rather than the number of bottles.

Thankfully, many price tags have unit prices written on them. If they don't, you can do a little iPhone math to calculate the unit price. Simply find out how many units you plan to purchase, and divide the total price by the number of units. So, if you bought a 12-ounce bottle of shampoo for $10, one unit of shampoo would cost $.83. This might sound tedious, but it is the only way to be sure that you are actually saving money with your bulk items, making it the first step in understanding how to buy in bulk.

Though you will be saving money in the long run, be prepared to throw down some cash upfront when you buy in bulk. You could easily spend $100 on bulk items in one go, but don't worry – they will last you weeks or even months, giving you plenty of time to save up (and polish off those 10 tubes of toothpaste).

1 What You Should Buy in Bulk. As a rule, you should buy things in bulk that save you money per unit, as mentioned above. When buying in bulk, saving money is the name of the game. In keeping with this mantra, you'll also want to reduce waste as much as possible. Because not using what you purchase is a waste of not only money but time and effort. Here are a few ways to go about avoiding waste when you buy in bulk.

B. Only buy what you need.

Have you ever walked into a grocery store for a single item and walked out with 20? The same thing can happen when you buy in bulk, only the costs will be much greater. For example, when you move into a new home it can be scary to see an empty fridge or pantry and there is the potential for you to buy too much too quickly. Sticking to the rule of only purchasing what you need can help you avoid situations such as this. No matter what you're shopping for, whether groceries, toiletries, or batteries, write a list of what you need, stay strong, and stick to it.

C. Choose items with a long shelf life.

If you want to get the most out of buying in bulk, make sure the items you buy will last for a while. Things like paper goods, dried pasta, and dried beans are great choices to buy in bulk. Perishable items like fruit and vegetables, on the other hand, can spoil quickly and if you do not plan to eat them within a week, you will want to avoid buying them in bulk. So if you're a family of two (opposed to six) you might want to hold off on buying 6 gallons of milk.

An important point to remember that in addition to food, other items can also expire. Liquid bleach loses its effectiveness after 6 to 12 months — even if you store it as directed, the contents can potentially lose potency over time. So to keep your whites really white, make sure you only buy enough bleach that you can use within 6 months. Here are some other household items that expire in less than 12 months:

Sunscreen

Tooth-whitening strips

Fabric softener

Over the counter medications

D. Buy items you're familiar with.

We know how frustrating it can be to buy a product that you can't wait to try, only to find that it does not live up to your expectations. Imagine having 10 bars of a new soap that you are allergic to, or 500 trash bags that do not fit your trash can. To save money, make sure that you are familiar with the items you buy in bulk before you purchase them.

E. Choose items that are on sale.

Try not to let discounts lure you into buying something you don't need, but if you see an item is already on your list *and* on sale – go for it! Stores selling bulk items often have sales and discounts year-round. The trick when you buy in bulk is not to let these "deals" distract you from what you really need. If something you need is already 25% cheaper per unit in bulk, and it is on sale, you will undoubtedly save money on an item you are already looking to buy.

1 Why moving is a Great Time to buy in bulk. A new home is like a fresh canvas, and moving gives you a chance to envision different storage and layout options before everything is set up. Additionally, it is much easier to see how much space you actually have *before* your home is filled with your personal belongings.

While you decide where your bed frame is going to go, you can designate certain spaces for any bulk items you plan to buy. If you have an extra closet, or even a large shelf available, you can plan for it to hold some of your bulk items. In setting this space aside, you can organize your belongings around your bulk items, ensuring that every item has a home.

You will also know very quickly whether or not you have the space for bulk purchases or if you should stick with smaller quantities. That said, do not opt for a larger home simply to fit your bulk buys. Know how to buy items in bulk that will fit your new home, not the other way around.

F.   When you have a small household.

It is easy to figure out how to buy in bulk for a family of four or more. Larger households tend to use more and go through food more quickly, so choosing to buy in bulk can save you multiple trips to the store. For households of three or less, you need to look more closely at your lifestyle, because buying in bulk could cost you more money over time if you aren't shopping smart.

G.   When you lack storage space.

If every corner of your home is occupied, or you live in a tiny apartment, you won't have the necessary space to store your bulk items. The same can be said if you are moving into a new home and want your linen closet to remain the designated towel spot. Rather than filling it with bulk items, you should do what is best for your household and hold off on buying in bulk.

H.   Before you move or travel.

There are plenty of things to do the month leading up to your move and, unless you are buying boxes, bulk buying should not top your moving checklist. Try to hold off and buy in bulk after your move is finalized, and then you can take everything directly to your new home. If you are looking for somewhere to start, we created a helpful grocery list for your new home —you can buy many of the items on this list in bulk.

The same goes for when you plan to travel. It might be tempting to stock up for your return, but it is best to wait until you get back from your trip to buy in bulk. Preparing for your trip will keep you busy enough without worrying about wasting food or unpacking your bulk items.

I. If you're forced to use your credit card.

Part of understanding how to buy in bulk knows how to budget. Buying in bulk can save you money in the long run, but it will generally cost you more money upfront. If you are not prepared to invest in bulk items, it might be best to wait until you are in a better financial position before embarking on the big shopping trip.

1 The Best Things to Buy in Bulk. As you become more comfortable with the best ways to buy in bulk, you will find yourself gravitating toward the right types of bulk items. Foods and supplies that have long shelf lives, and are generally cheaper per unit, are great items to buy in bulk. Here are a few examples of the types of things you should regularly buy in bulk:

Butter

Alcohol

Batteries

School and office supplies

Paper products

Laundry detergent

Toothpaste

Trash bags

Gift cards

Lightbulbs

Shipping/moving boxes

Packing tape

Diapers

Things Never to Buy in Bulk

When you have extra space, it might be tempting to try and fill your pantry, fridge, and closets with as much stuff as possible. Try to resist the urge to buy certain things in bulk, however, as it could cost you more money in the long run. As mentioned above, perishable foods, brands you've never tried, and items that do not save you money should all be avoided. You might be surprised by some of the items on this list since, despite popular opinion, all of these items do inspire:

Bleach

Spices

Olive oil

Eggs

Sunscreen

Canned veggies

Condiments

Fresh produce

How to Buy in Bulk for Your Bathroom

The good news is that most of the things you need for your bathroom can be bought in bulk. Here is a list of some great bulk items you can buy for your bathroom:

Toothpaste

Toilet paper

Toothbrushes and toothbrush heads

Shampoo

Soap

Tissues

Lint rollers

Glass and tile cleaner

Floss

Nail polish remover

Shaving foam

Air freshener

Before you shop, first look at the storage space you have and see how you can maximize the space. Can you add shelves or dividers under the sink? Can you install a medicine cabinet? Is there space in your linen closet for extra supplies? If so, go ahead and pick up the items you need the most and that will fit comfortably in your bathroom. Toothpaste and toothbrushes are great buys because they will last months or years, and can easily fit in small spaces.

2 How to Buy in Bulk for Your Kitchen When figuring out how to buy in bulk for your kitchen, be aware of the size of your household and how much you consume on a regular basis. If you choose food items, make sure your whole family likes them and that they have a long shelf life. These are some of the best items you can buy in bulk for your kitchen:

Sponges

Dish soap

Garbage bags

Paper towels

Dishwasher detergent

Surface cleaner

Foil

Plastic wrap

Wax paper

Sandwich and freezer bags

Antibacterial wipes

Coffee filters

Parchment

K-cups

Bottled water

How to Buy in Bulk for Your Office

Whether you are restocking your home office or buying for a larger business space, rest assured that you will have a hard time running out of supplies when you buy them in bulk. Here are some of the best items to buy in bulk for your office:

Staples

Paper clips

Pushpins

Printer paper

Printer ink

Printer toner

Pens

Pencils

Scissors

Hand sanitizer

Sticky notes

Legal notepads and notebooks

Binder clips

Lightbulbs

Gum

J.   Use coupons.

Coupons can save you even more money when you buy in bulk. Take a few minutes to search for coupons online or in the store's catalog, and take them with you on your next bulk shopping trip. You might even be able to save a few up to get a really good deal or combine them with an in-store discount.

K.   Share with your friends.

If you are a small family or live in a tiny space, you can get some friends together to share the items you buy in bulk. Splitting a 12-pound bag of rice, for instance, between yourself and two of your friends will leave each of you with a more manageable quantity. By dividing the costs, only taking home what you need, and keeping what fits comfortably in your home, you can save money, avoid waste, and maximize space.

L.   Don't forgo quality for a cheap price.

Getting a good deal is only a good deal when you get something for less than it is worth. This is especially important when you buy clothes in bulk. Do not be tempted to buy a lower quality item to save money in the short term when you will only have to replace it after a few washes. Trust us, it's worth paying a little bit extra for a t-shirt that does not fade in the wash, or socks that make it through the entire season.

Knowing how to buy in bulk can make life a lot easier when you are either moving or just looking to save a little extra cash. Keep this guide handy when you buy in bulk, to make sure you save time, money, and space by choosing the best items and shopping smart.

Reduce your utility bills

Electricity, gas, and other utilities can deeply impact your monthly budget if you let them. So don't. Be smart about ways to keep your home cool during the summer and warm during winter. You may even consider investing in or building solar panels to channel the sun's natural energy into electricity. Keep your utilities low, and watch the money you save start to mount.

According to the U.S. Department of Energy, the typical American family spends over $1,600.00 a year on utilities. We all could probably save significant amounts on our utilities by buying the newest and most efficient appliances, heaters and boilers. But the amount of money we'd have to pay upfront is sometimes prohibitive, and it's difficult to be sure that long-term reductions in our utility bills would be worth it.

The good news is that the concept of snowflaking is particularly well-suited to helping us cope with climate control. Below are 20 ideas that, for a reasonable cost, can help us reduce the amount we pay each year for water, electricity and heat/cooling.

1 Get an Energy-use Consultation: In many communities, utilities companies provide this service for free, or for a nominal fee. Many local volunteer organizations also perform energy audits. They can test your home to identify your areas of greatest heating/cooling loss, analyze your past utility bills, and, in some cases, estimate how long it would take you to recoup the cost of upgrades to your home or apartment. If you'd rather perform your own audit, the Department of Energy has an online audit tool that takes you through the steps.

2 Install Extra Insulation: This can be expensive, but it doesn't have to be, especially considering that attics, basements/crawl spaces, and the areas around utility pipes can be some of the

biggest heat suckers in your home. These areas are usually tucked out of sight anyway, so the insulation job you do doesn't have to be pretty, it just has to be effective and safe. Also, remember that insulation will help you even if you live in the tropics. Not only does it keep in warm air when it's cold, it keeps in cool air when it's hot.

3 Seal Off Gaps: **Weather stripping, heat-safe tape, and caulk are all relatively inexpensive and easy to find. Use them to seal off leaks to the outside of your home. Two things to pay attention to in your quest to mind your gaps: 1) The Department of Energy estimates that only 10% of air loss in a typical house comes from windows, whereas 15% comes from ducts and 13% comes from plumbing leading outside or to other un-insulated areas. 2) Ducts especially are tricky creatures, and sealing or insulating them improperly can be hazardous. Make sure that you know what you're doing, or talk to someone who does, before you tamper with them.**

4 Install Door Sweeps: **If you have several heating zones in your house, installing small, insulating door sweeps on the bottom of your doors can help keep those zones from leaking into one another. Even if you don't have zones, installing door sweeps on your outside doors, and the doors closest to the outside, can cut down on air leakage. Sweeps are easy to install, and cost about $5-$10 dollars.**

5 Get a Programmable Thermostat and Use it: **Now that the above steps are complete, and you aren't leaking energy like a sieve, this step is the equivalent of having part of your paycheck automatically sent to your savings account. Set the thermostat a few degrees lower while you're away at work, and a few degrees lower yet for bedtime. If you have multiple heat zones in your house, even better. Chances are some of those zones won't need to be heated up to livable temperatures 24-7. If you live in an area where central a/c is required, some of the same conditions apply. The house can probably be 85 degrees in the daytime while you're away at work. These thermostats can be**

expensive, but they offer significant savings as well. Amazon offers a wide selection of programmable thermostats, many for under $50.

6 Consider a Heated Mattress Pad: **If you live in an area with cold winters, you can probably turn your thermostat down even more during the night by using one of these. The electricity that it takes to heat your bed is minuscule compared to the cost of heating your entire house a few extra degrees at night.**

7 Use Compact-Fluorescent Bulbs: **Yes, the light they give off is different from that of normal incandescent bulbs. But they typically use 75% less energy, and last ten times as long.**

8 Use Power Strips: **Even in sleep mode, your computer, DVD player, and other electronic devices use some energy. By plugging them into power strips, and then turning off the power at the strip, you use less electricity.**

9 Maintain/Clean Your Appliances: **If your heating vents (or the vents on the underside of your baseboard heater) are caked in dust, they probably aren't running at maximum efficiency. Likewise, replace or clean the filter on your furnace and drain the sediment from your water heater as often as their user manuals say you should. Appliances last longer when they're well-maintained, and it will knock some money off your utilities as well.**

10 Make Your Water Heater More Efficient: **If it's an old heater, chances are it's not as well-insulated as it could be. (Though be sure to first check the owner's manual to see if it's safe to add an insulating cover to your water heater.) Most hardware stores sell insulating sleeves for water heaters for around $20-$30. Likewise, make sure the pipes leading from your heater to the wall are insulated. If they're not, simple pipe insulation, again available at most hardware stores, should do the trick.**

11 Turn Down your Water Heater: **If your water heater is set at 140 degrees or above, chances are that you can get away with**

only set it at 120. The only thing you might need 140-degree water for is your dishwasher. Experiment a bit and see if you can get clean dishes at lower temperatures.

12 Install Faucet Aerators: **They use less water, even if you're turning on the taps for the same amount of time. You should be able to get faucet aerators for less than two dollars apiece. Chances are you already have some form of the aerator in your faucet (they're those little mesh screen pieces that screw onto the nozzle). If you already have them, you can unscrew them and check the side for their GPM (gallons per minute) rating. If it's over 2.75 gallons, it's probably worth it to get one with a better, lower rating.**

13 Install a Low-flow Shower Head: **If you take long showers, this is definitely an investment to think about. These puppies cost anywhere from $5 to $50. Most of them operate by aerating the water. Note that low-flow showerheads should not reduce your water-pressure by all that much. Take a look at your local hardware store's return policy, too. It might be worth it to experiment with several different types if you can return them after one or two uses.**

14 Only Run Your Dishwasher When Full: **Unless you have a newer dishwasher with a half-wash option, you use the same amount of water no matter how many dishes you put in. Also note that since it's hot water, you're paying not only for H2O but also for the energy used to heat it.**

15 Air-dry Dishes: **Instead of using the drying cycle on your dishwasher, just set it to clean only, and open the door when the dishwasher is done. The wire racks in the dishwasher can conveniently double as drying racks, and you'll save the energy it would have taken to dry all your dishes.**

16 Wash Whites on Warm, Not hot: **Unless you or a member of your household is an athlete, or particularly stinky, your whites will probably turn out just as clean on the warm setting as they**

did on the hot setting, and you save your water heater from having to heat up several gallons of water to max temperature.

17 Simulate a Low Flush Toilet: **If you don't have a new, water-saver toilet, you can simulate one by putting a clean brick, or a sealed plastic bottle filled with pebbles, or a weighted mason jar, into your toilet tank. This displaces water so that less is used each time you flush.**

18 Be Kind to Your Freezer/Refrigerator: **Let hot food sit out an hour or so before you put it in the fridge so that you don't waste energy having your fridge work extra hard to cool it down. If you have empty space in your freezer and live in a cool place, freeze plastic containers full of water by putting them outside, and then put them into your empty freezer space, giving the freezer a helping hand.**

19 Buy Wisely: **When Buying New Appliances, pay attention to their energy ratings: An Energy Star logo is put on many appliances that meet federal standards for energy efficiency. Large appliances such as refrigerators, boilers, water heaters, dishwashers, etc. have yellow Energy Guide tags on them that tell you how energy efficient an appliance is compared to other models.**

20 Consider Tax Breaks/Energy Incentives: **Your county or state may have an initiative that offers savings on certain energy-efficient appliances. Rebates may be available for large, expensive appliances that meet certain energy requirements. Check the Database of State Incentives for Renewables and Efficiency to learn more about options in your state. The database also includes a federal incentives page.**

Bonus Tip: **Pay your utility bills with your cashback credit card. Many utilities let you pay with a credit card, and you can also pay your phone, internet and cable bills with a cashback card, too. It's a convenient way to pay your bills and an easy way to pocket some cash each month. Our favorite cash** back card is the Chase Freedom, which offers up to 5% cash back and a $150 Bonus Cash Back for new cardholders.

Get a home energy audit

This will allow you to find out how many dollars are seeping out of your home in the form of lost energy.

You can perform your own energy audit if you're the industrious type, but don't hesitate to hire a professional to complete the audit for you. It should cost anywhere from $300 to $500, which isn't cheap, but it could help you save much more than that over time (especially if you decide to re-insulate the home).

While a professional home energy audit is the best way to determine where your home is losing energy and where you can save, you can conduct your own simple but diligent walk-through and spot many problems in any type of house. This "do-it-yourself" home energy audit will not be as thorough as a professional home energy assessment, but it can help you pinpoint some of the easier areas to address. When walking through your home, keep a checklist of areas you have inspected and problems you found. This list will help you prioritize your energy efficiency upgrades. Do not assume that just because your home is recently constructed—or even new—that there are no opportunities to save energy. Energy-saving technology has evolved rapidly over the past few years, outpacing training commonly available to many builders, including some of the most reputable.

A. Locate Air Leaks

First, make a list of obvious air leaks (drafts). The potential energy savings from reducing drafts in a home may range from 10% to 20% per year, and the home is generally much more comfortable afterward.

Check for indoor air leaks, such as gaps along the baseboard or edge of the flooring and at junctures of the walls and ceiling. Also check for leaks on the outside of your home, especially in areas where two different building materials meet. Other places to check for leaks include windows, doors, lighting and plumbing fixtures, switches, and electrical outlets. Also check for open fireplace dampers. See Detecting air leaks for detailed instructions on finding air leaks yourself.

B. Seal Air Leaks

You should plug and caulk holes or penetrations for faucets, pipes, electric outlets, and wiring. Look for cracks and holes in the mortar, foundation, and siding, and look for leaks around windows and doors. Seal them with the appropriate material. Learn more about selecting and applying caulk and weather-stripping.

C. Consider Ventilation

When sealing any home, you must always be aware of the danger of indoor air pollution and combustion appliance "backdrafts." Backdrafting is when the various combustion appliances and exhaust fans in the home compete for air. An exhaust fan may pull the combustion gases back into the living space. This can obviously create a very dangerous and unhealthy situation in the home.

In homes where a fuel is burned (i.e., natural gas, fuel oil, propane, or wood) for heating, be certain the appliance has an adequate air supply. Generally, one square inch of vent opening is required for each 1,000 Btu of appliance input heat. Burn marks or soot around the appliance burner or at the vent collar, or visible smoke anywhere in the utility room while the appliance is operating, indicate poor draft. When in doubt, contact your local utility company, energy professional, or ventilation contractor. Learn more about proper ventilation.

D. Check Insulation

Heat loss through the ceiling and walls in your home could be very large if the insulation levels are less than the recommended minimum. When your house was built, the builder likely installed the amount of insulation recommended at that time. Given today's energy prices (and future prices that will probably be higher), the level of insulation might be inadequate, especially if you have an older home.

If the attic hatch is located above a conditioned space, check to see if it is at least as heavily insulated as the attic, is weather stripped, and closes tightly. In the attic, determine whether openings for items such as pipes, ductwork, and chimneys are sealed. Seal any gaps with an expanding foam caulk or some other permanent sealant. When sealing gaps around chimneys or other heat-producing devices, be sure to use a non-combustible sealant.

While you are inspecting the attic, check to see if there is a vapor barrier under the attic insulation. The vapor barrier might be tarpaper, Kraft paper attached to fiberglass batts, or a plastic sheet. If there does not appear to be a vapor barrier, you might consider painting the interior ceilings with vapor barrier paint. This reduces the amount of water vapor that can pass through the ceiling. Large amounts of moisture can reduce the effectiveness of insulation and promote structural damage.

Make sure that the attic vents are not blocked by insulation. You also should seal any electrical boxes in the ceiling with flexible caulk (from the living room side or attic side) and cover the entire attic floor with at least the current recommended amount of insulation.

Checking a wall's insulation level is more difficult. Select an exterior wall and turn off the circuit breaker or unscrew the fuse for any outlets in the wall. Be sure to test the outlets to make certain that they are not "hot." Check the outlet by plugging in a functioning lamp or portable radio. Once you are sure your outlets are not getting any electricity, remove the cover plate from one of the outlets and gently probe into the wall with a thin, long stick or screwdriver. A plastic crochet hook is particularly suited, as it will retrieve small bits of any insulation material for easy identification. If you encounter a slight resistance, you have some insulation there. You could also make a small hole in a closet, behind a couch, or in some other unobtrusive place to see what, if anything, the wall cavity is filled with. Ideally, the wall cavity should be totally filled with some form of insulation material. Unfortunately, this method cannot tell you if the entire wall is insulated, or if the insulation has settled. Only a thermographic inspection can do this.

If your basement or crawlspace is unconditioned and open to the exterior, determine whether there is insulation under the living area flooring. In most areas of the country, an R-value of 25 is the recommended minimum level of insulation. If the sub-space is enclosed and contains heating or cooling appliances, air ducts or plumbing, you should probably insulate the subspace perimeter rather than the living space floor. The insulation at the top of the foundation wall and first-floor perimeter should have an R-value of 19 or greater. If the basement is intentionally conditioned, the foundation walls should also be insulated to at least R-19. Your water heater, hot water pipes, and furnace ducts should all be insulated. For more information, see our insulation section.

E. Inspect Heating and Cooling Equipment

Inspect heating and cooling equipment annually, or as recommended by the manufacturer. If you have a forced-air furnace, check your filters and replace them as needed. Generally, you should change them about once every month or two, especially during periods of high usage. Have a professional check and clean your equipment once a year.

If the unit is more than 15 years old, you should consider replacing your system with one of the newer, energy-efficient units. A new unit would greatly reduce your energy consumption, especially if the existing equipment is in poor condition. Check your ductwork for dirt streaks, especially near seams. These indicate air leaks, and they should be sealed with a duct mastic. Insulate any ducts or pipes that travel through unheated spaces. An insulation R-Value of 6 is the recommended minimum.

F. Lighting

Energy for lighting accounts for about 10% of your electric bill. Examine the light bulbs in your house and consider replacing inefficient bulbs with a more efficient choice, such as energy-saving incandescents, compact fluorescent lamps (CFLs), or light-emitting diodes (LEDs). When shopping for bulbs, consider the brightness of the bulbs you want and look for lumens and the Lighting Facts label. Your electric utility may offer rebates or other incentives for purchasing energy-efficient lamps. Also look for ways to use controls such as sensors, dimmers, or timers to reduce lighting use.

G. Appliances and Electronics

The appliances and electronics you choose and how you use them affect your energy use and costs. Examine the appliances and electronics in your home and estimate their energy use. Consider strategies for reducing the energy use of your appliances and electronics.

H. You might consider the following:

Unplugging an item when it is not in use to prevent phantom loads

Changing the settings or using the item less often

Purchasing a new, more efficient product. Learn more about shopping for efficient appliances and electronics.

Your Whole-House Plan

After you know where your home is losing energy, make a plan by asking yourself a few questions:

How much money do you spend on energy?

Where are your greatest energy losses?

How long will it take for an investment in energy efficiency to pay for itself in energy cost savings?

Do the energy-saving measures provide additional benefits that are important to you—for example, increased comfort from installing double-paned, efficient windows?

CHAPTER NO 4: SAVING MONEY

Pay yourself first.

This means before you go and blow your paycheck on a new pair of shoes or a golf club you don't need, put money aside in an account that you don't touch. Do this every time you get paid and watch your account grow.

The phrase "pay yourself first" has become increasingly popular in personal finance and investing circles. Instead of paying all your bills and expenses first and then saving whatever is left over, do the opposite. Set aside money for investing, retirement, college, a down payment, or whatever requires a long-term effort, and *then* take care of everything else.

A. Determining Your Current Spending

1 Determine your monthly income. Before paying yourself first, you need to figure out how much to pay yourself. Determining this begins with taking a look at your current monthly income. To determine monthly income, simply add together all your income sources for the month.

Note that this is a net amount or take-home income after deductions from paycheck or applicable taxes.

If you have an income that fluctuates from month to month, use your average income over the past six months, or a number slightly below average to represent your monthly income. It is always better to choose a lower number, that way you're more likely to end up with more income than planned, rather than less.

2 Determine your monthly expenses. The easiest way to determine monthly spending is to simply look at your banking records for the past month. Simply add together any bill

payments, cash withdrawals, or money transfers. Be sure to include any cash payments you received that were spent as well.

There are two basic types of expenses to be aware of — fixed expenses, and variable expenses. Your fixed expenses stay the same month-to-month and typically include things like rent, utilities, phone/internet, debt repayments or insurance. Variable expenses change month-to-month and may include food, entertainment, gasoline, or miscellaneous purchases.

If tracking your expenses manually is too challenging, consider using software like Mint (or the many others like it). With Mint, you simply sync your bank accounts with the software, and the software will track your spending for you, by category. This gives you a clear, organized, and up-to-date vision of your spending.

3 Subtract your monthly income from your monthly expenses. Subtracting monthly income from expenses lets you know how much leftover money you have at the end of each month. This is important to know, since it can help you to determine how much to pay yourself first. You would not want to pay yourself first and then discover you are lacking money for important fixed expenses.

If your monthly income is $2,000 per month, and your total expenses are $1,600, you technically have $400 to pay yourself first with. This gives you a good baseline idea of how much you may be able to save each month.

Note this number can potentially be much higher. Once you know the current amount of leftover money you have, you can take steps to reduce expenses to make this figure even higher.

If you are negative at the end of the month, reducing expenses will become even more important.

B. Creating a Budget Based on Lower Expenses

1 Look to reduce your fixed expenses. Fixed expenses may be fixed, but that does not mean you can't replace them with lower fixed expenses. Take a look at each type of fixed expense and examine if there are any ways to reduce them.

For example, your cell phone bill may be fixed every month, but is it possible to drop down to a plan with lower data to save money? Similarly, your rent may also be fixed, but if your rent takes up more than half of your income, you should examine perhaps downgrading from a two-bedroom to a one-bedroom apartment if possible, or relocating to a more affordable area.

If you have car insurance, be sure to contact your broker each year to see if there are better deals available, or alternatively, continually shop around for better deals.

If you have high levels of expensive credit card debt, consider a debt consolidation loan to reduce your fixed interest expense each month. This will allow you to pay off your credit card debt with a lower interest rate consolidation loan.

2 Look to reduce your variable expenses. This is where most savings can be found. Take a close look at your expenses each month and see where your spending that is not towards fixed expenses goes. Look at small expenses that add up over time like coffee purchases, eating out, grocery bills, gasoline, or leisure purchases.

When looking to reduce these expenses, think about what you want, versus what you need. Look to cut out as many wants as possible. For example, you may need to have lunch every day at work, but purchasing lunch at the cafeteria is a want. You could select the more affordable option of making lunch each day.

The key is to look at variable expense areas that take up a large portion of your budget. Is most of your extra spending on gasoline, food, entertainment, or impulse purchases? You could target reductions in those areas by using more public transport, packing more lunches for work, opting for more affordable entertainment choices, or leaving your credit card at home to reduce impulse spending, for example.

Do an online search to find innovative ways to reduce your variable expenses in areas you struggle with.

3 Calculate how much money you have leftover after making reductions. If you have identified a few areas to reduce your spending, subtract that amount from your expenses. You can then subtract the new expense amount from your monthly income to determine how much you have leftover.

Assume monthly income is $2,000, and your expenses were $1,600. After looking for expense reductions, you may have managed to find $200 in savings each month, bringing your monthly expenses down to $1,400. You now have $600 leftover each month.

C. Paying Yourself First

1 Decide how much to pay yourself. Now that you know how much you have leftover, you can decide how much to pay yourself. Experts recommend differing amounts. In the famous personal finance book The Wealthy Barber, the author David Chilton recommends paying yourself 10% of your net or take-home income. Other experts recommend anywhere between 1% and 5%.

The best solution is to pay yourself as much as you can based on your leftover amount each month. For example, if you have $600 leftover at the end of the month, and your income is $2,000, you would be able to save up to 30% of your income. (You may only want to put 20% of that in savings, leaving yourself a little wiggle room for unexpected treats or expenses.)

2 Set a savings goal. Once you know how much you can possibly pay yourself, try to set a goal for a savings amount. For example, your goal may be retirement, education savings, or a house down-payment. Determine the cost of your goal, and divide that by the amount you can pay yourself monthly to determine how long it will take to attain in months.

For example, you may want to save for a $50,000 home down payment. If you have $600 leftover every month and choose to save $300 of that, it would take you a very long 13 years to save $50,000.

In that case, you could boost your savings amount to $600 to drop the time in half (since you have $600 leftover).

Keep in mind that if you invest your money in a high-interest savings account, or in other types of investments, the return you get would further shorten your time. To figure out how fast your saving amount will grow at a certain rate of return (say 2% per year), go online, and search "Compound Interest Calculator."

3 Create an account that is separate from all your other accounts. This account should be only for a specified goal, usually saving or investing. If possible, choose an account with a higher interest rate — usually these types of accounts limit how often you can withdraw money, which is a good thing because you're not going to be pulling money out of it, anyway.

Consider opening a high-interest savings account. Many institutions offer these, and they typically pay rates that are well above a checking account.

You can also consider opening a Roth IRA for your savings. Roth IRA's allow your wealth to grow tax-free over time. Within a Roth IRA, you can purchase stocks, mutual funds, bonds, or exchange-traded funds, and these products all offer the opportunity to earn a higher return than a high-interest savings account.

Other options include traditional IRAs or a 401(k).

4 Put that money into the account as soon as it is available. If you have direct deposit, have a portion of each paycheck automatically deposited into the separate account. You can also set up an automatic monthly or weekly transfer from your main, active account to your separate account if you can keep track of your balance enough to avoid overdraft fees. The point is to do this before you spend money on anything else, including bills and rent.

5 Leave the money alone. Don't touch it. Don't pull money out of it. You should have a separate emergency fund for just that — emergencies. Typically that fund should be enough to cover you for three to six months. Do not confuse an emergency fund with a saving or investing fund. If you find that you don't have enough money to pay your bills, look for other ways to make money or cut expenses. Don't charge them on your credit card (see Warnings below).

Make a budget (and stick to it)

Create a monthly budget that covers all of your basic expenses and leaves a little bit of "fun" money aside. Sticking by your budget and saving at least some money each month is a good way to lay the groundwork for your efforts to get rich.

Budgeting money is important for us to be able to meet our expenses whether in the home or business, manage our money, and keep our finances in check. We need to know where our money is going, and put away enough to pay for our monthly bills. It is important for every bit of our income to be accounted for so that we are aware of where we might be spending too much, and where we can cut back so that our most important expenses are covered at the end of the month.

A. Creating Your Budget

1 Record the net monthly income that you receive. Net income is the amount that you actually get to take home, after all the deductions (taxes, health care) have been subtracted. Include other sources of income as well if applicable, such as tips, monthly bonuses, cost of living increases, dividends, interest income, etc.

What do you do if your income is constantly changing? You pretty much have to do things topsy-turvy. Determine all your essential, priority, and lifestyle expenses first. Then, with your paycheck, start paying off all your essential needs first, followed by your priority and then lifestyle expenses. The money you have leftover can either be set aside for an emergency account or stashed away into savings.

2 Remove from your net monthly income your stated savings goal. Ideally, set up an automatic withdrawal into another account so that you aren't even tempted to touch it. If you never see it, you won't miss it. Squirreling away savings will help

you anticipate emergency scenarios and prepare you for retirement.

How much money should you try to save? It mostly depends on your salary, but a good benchmark is 15% to 20%. If you can only afford to save 10% of your annual income, that's fine, provided that you save some of it.

Take advantage of matching contributions from your employer, if possible. If your employer matches contributions to your 401(k) — up to a certain percent — take full advantage of their generosity. It's the closest thing you'll get to "free money" in your lifetime.

3 List down your monthly expenses into three separate categories. These categories are "fixed," "flexible," and "discretionary."

Fixed expenses remain the same each month, such as a mortgage or rent, a loan payment, insurance or medical premiums, etc. Total up all fixed expenses.

Flexible expenses include items that are necessary, but in which you can control the amount of money spent on, such as household and grocery items, clothing, utilities, etc. Total up all flexible expenses.

Discretionary expenses are items that are not necessary for survival. These could include expenses for recreation such as movies, travels, and impulse buys. If your expense to income ratio is out of balance and you are spending more money than you earn, items from this category should be eliminated or cut back.Total up all discretionary expenses.

4 Subtract the total amount of expenses from the total income for the month. If the expense total is less than the income total, then you are managing your finances well and should keep up with doing so. But if the expense total is greater than the income total, you are off-track financially and need to prioritize expenses.

5 If your budget is feeling pinched, take a look at flexible and discretionary expenses. Check your bank and credit statement to see what you spend money on, or sign up for a personal finance application online. This will help you track what you spend money on that's not absolutely essential.

Keep track of when you use credit cards. Did you know that people who use credit cards are more likely to spend more money than people who use cold, hard cash? That's because cash "feels" more real, so it hurts more than credit. Try carrying only cash around and see if you spend less.

Look to see how much you spend on eating out, on your morning coffee from Starbucks, on watching movies in the cinema, and other costs you can cut back on. Many people need their Starbucks fix, even if there's a coffee machine at work. One cup of coffee per day, at $2.50 per cup, equals more than $900 per year! Think about what you could do with $900.

Begin to have the tough discussions about what you can cut back on or cut out altogether. Whether this conversation is made with a spouse or with yourself, try to be honest, forthright, and understanding. Nobody likes cutting back spending, even if it needs to be done.

6 Look at how much money you now have left from your income, after the expenses have been covered for. This is the only amount that is yours to spend if you aim to be debt-free. If you get paid weekly, make sure enough money is set aside to meet the monthly bills. Never borrow from the amount that should be used for monthly expenses. This reserve method will save you from living paycheck to paycheck.

7 Review the budget plan during the end of each income period, in order to ensure that you stay on track. Compare actual expenses against what you budgeted. If there are glaring

variances, you might need to make adjustments on your discretionary expenses. As time passes, you may want to only perform this comparison on a quarterly basis.

B. Sticking to Your Budget

1 Seek out technological help. If you're the old-school type who loves to balance their checkbook, more power to you! But know that emerging technology is making it easier than ever to track your expenses in real-time, and with more sophisticated software. Mint.com, Quicken, and wallet.ai are all-powerful online tools that will help you keep track of expenses and budget for the future.

2 Don't give it all up at the first sign of failure. Budgeting is like dieting. A lot of people start with majestic intentions. Then, when they fail to see results within two months, or when they start getting bored, they throw their hands up and quit, telling themselves it's not worth it. Don't give up before the battle has even started. Prepare yourself by acknowledging that budgets take a lot of time and a little effort.

Try to give yourself a full year of budgeting to determine whether it makes any difference in your finances. If, after a year of steady, scrupulous budgeting, it still hasn't made a dent in your savings or put a wad of cash in your pocket, feel free to re-evaluate. You won't be disappointed.

3 Start contributing to an emergency fund. No, an emergency fund is not the same thing as your savings fund. An emergency fund is 6 to 12 months' worth of living expenses, frittered away for — you guessed it — an emergency. What if you lose your job? What if your daughter needs to go to the hospital? A host of emergencies can potentially burn a hole in your pocket. Being prepared is the best step and one that makes a difference in your budget.

4 Spend your tax refund wisely. A tax refund, if you're entitled to it, can be a huge windfall. Imagine getting a thousand, or two thousand dollars, without really expecting it. Knowing how to spend this potential windfall, however, can be pretty tricky, especially if you're barely above water. Think about contributing to your emergency or savings fund instead of spending it on a new flat-screen TV.

5 Pay off your debts slowly but surely. According to AARP, American households hold an average of $8,400 in debt. That's a lot of cheese — a lot of cheese you owe somebody else. If you happen to pay off your debt each month with your income, that's great. But if you're like many other people, you might be struggling to pay off your debts each month, meaning that you have to attack things a little more strategically.

Which debts to you pay off first? High-interest debt or low interest-debt? Attacking low-interest debt and paying off certain debt lines altogether is called "snowballing." Attacking high-interest debt first is called "avalanching."

If you're highly-motivated to pay off debts, go for avalanching. High-interest debts can gather up lots of compound interest fast, making this approach ultimately cheaper. If you need help motivating yourself, however, you might want to try snowballing, even if it means you'll pay more.

Downgrade your car and house

Could you make do with an apartment instead of a house, or have roommates instead of your own place? Could you buy a used car instead of a new one and use it more sparingly? These are all ways to save a ton of money every month

You've made the decision to live without a car. Congratulations! While a car is a useful solution to getting from place to place, it can also cost a lot of money to maintain. Cars can also cause a lot of unneeded stress. Without one, you'll save time and money while getting healthier at the same time. Say goodbye to road rage, gas and traffic, and embrace your new calmer, more peaceful (and more money-filled) life.

A. Biking for Success

1 Choose a bike. There are many different types of bikes to choose from. It's important to pick the one that will best serve your needs. Consider your traveling distance, the terrain, and the grade you'll be riding when you choose your model.

Visit a bike show and talk to the employees. Check out what they have to offer. Take the models you like out for a test spin around the block.

Consider how you'll be using the bike. If you're using the bike to go back and forth to work, to the grocery store, and to run other errands on the pavement, consider a road bike, which is quick, efficient, and light.

Determine if a mountain bike is a sound investment. They are durable and can jump easily from pavement to mud and sand. They are built to take a thrashing. They're just not that great for endurance rides.

Consider the weight of the bike. It might not seem very heavy going for a spin around the block. It will be much heavier as you pedal it through miles on your way home from work. Buying a lighter frame will make the ride home much more manageable.

2 Buy a bike. Keep your budget in mind. Classifieds and online sources are a great place to begin. Also, ask a friend if they have a bike they'd be willing to sell.

Get a bike multi-tool, tire patches, a spare tire, lube, and a flashlight. Keep them in your riding bag in case of an emergency.

Buy a bike lock and use it. Talk to someone at a bike store to find out what will work best for you. Always use multiple locking mechanisms. Although not foolproof, a kryptonite U-lock with a four-foot long cable is a good way to prevent bike thieves.

Get bad weather gear. You've gotten rid of your car, so you'll be exposed to the elements on your rides home. Being prepared means a smooth ride.

Buying a waterproof bag to keep your equipment in will help you out. Check for used ones online for the best deal.

3 Take care of your bike. Bikes, like cars, need proper maintenance. A small amount of care can make all the difference in your ride.

Learn how to take care of your bike. Your bike is a series of moving parts. Learn each of these moving parts and what they do. When you expose them to the elements like rain, mud, sand, or snow, the parts will begin to deteriorate. A few simple steps can save you a breakdown in the middle of your commute.

Do a pre-ride inspection. Like a car, you will benefit from making sure there are no glaring problems to hinder your ride before you begin pedaling. Check the tires, for any loose parts, the chain, and the brakes.

Clean your bike. Wipe it all over with a dry rag. Take note of any loose parts. Base your cleaning schedule on how often you ride. If you ride every day, wipe your bike down every few.

Secure any loose bolts. Don't over tighten them by cranking down on them.

Apply lube to protect moving parts (the chain, the brake and derailleur levers, the brake and derailleur cables, the brake and derailleur assemblies, and the bearing systems) from the natural wear and tear of riding. It will keep rust and corrosion at bay. Don't over-lubricate as too much will attract dirt and debris.

4 Secure your bike. Many bikes are stolen because they are not properly secured. Becoming familiar with how to lock your bike up will help give you some piece of mind as you are going about your day.

Always use your bike lock. A good lock is your first line of defense against would-be bike thieves.

Know how to lock your bike. Put your cable through your frame and both wheels. The U-lock goes through the back wheel (inside the rear triangle of the frame). Secure the bike to something solid. This approach locks the rear wheel and the frame.

The smaller the U-lock the better. It's easier to carry around and is harder to break.

Consider the insurance quality bike locks offer. You can fill out a form online after purchase, and in the event someone steals your bike, they will pay your homeowners or renters insurance deductible or they will pay to replace the bike. Research your options. Don't throw any receipts away (for the bike, the locks, or the tools).

5 Find a safe place to park your bike. If you can, take it inside with you and find a safe place to store it while you're away. Make sure to lock it when you are not around, even if it's just for a short time.

Use a small U-lock if you lock your bike to a parking meter, never just a cable. A small U-lock makes it impossible to lift the bike over the top.

Look for immovable bike racks installed outside of buildings. Check to make sure it's bolted down and solid. Never lock your bike to something flimsy, like a chain-link fence that can be easily snipped open.

Look for parking garages and parking lots that are bike-friendly. While some ask for a minimal fee, it's worth the cost for peace of mind.

Bring your bike inside when you return home if you can. If you can't, secure your bike with as much precaution as you would when you take it out. Even if you're tired, taking these extra steps will help ensure you have a ride tomorrow.

Bring any accessories with you after parking your bike: lights, water bottles, seat, etc.

Take care of yourself, too. A soggy-wet, cold bike ride is miserable. Dress to stay dry. Buy a waterproof vest or jacket with a hood. Rain pants are always a great investment.

B. Taking the Bus

1 Find out the bus routes in your city and plan your route. They should be available online. If not, ask the bus driver and he/she

should be able to help. Don't be afraid to ask, especially if you are using multiple transfers.

Learn how to use a transfer ticket. A transfer will allow the passengers to board a second bus or train going in the same direction to complete their trip. Transfers are generally free (check online or call the transit center for transfer prices) and can be requested at the time of payment. Transfers are generally only available one-way. Also, you may have to wait for the next line when you transfer, so schedule extra time to complete your trip.

Master the pickup times. Time how long it takes you to walk from home to the station. Subtract that time from the pickup time and you'll know exactly when you need to leave the house. Give yourself a few minutes on both ends.

Keep the transit systems number in your phone so you can call to check the times in case of inclement weather or traffic delays. Often transit systems have apps you can download onto your phone that are very helpful. Take advantage of these if you can.

2 Bring exact change. They don't offer change, so this part is up to you. Having it in your hand as your board will make the exchange as pleasant as possible.

Consider buying a pass. In many cases, there are discounted bus passes to people. Check out the costs online and do the math to see whether it's cheaper to buy a month or year-long pass.

3 Bring your own entertainment. Using transit means you have extra time to yourself. Use this time for something you enjoy!

Bring a book. Buying cheap paperbacks at the thrift store is economical and fun. You can also invest in a reading pad and download books for free from your local library.

Bring your own music. Download music through your phone or buy an iPod. Older models are very inexpensive online and can be used just for downloading music. Make sure to keep the volume at a level that won't bother your surrounding neighbors.

Listen to a radio program. There are many great apps to download so you won't miss your favorite radio show now that you don't have a car. Download them, sit back, and enjoy your time.

4 Be polite. Use your best manners and treat everyone with courtesy and respect. Good manners are contagious and they can keep bad manners at bay.

Keep your bag in your lap. Don't spread your stuff out.

Don't eat on the bus. Just don't. Wait until you get out.

Offer your seat if someone older or otherwise infirm boards. It's a polite and respectful thing to do.

Say thank you to your transit driver. It might be the thing that keeps them waiting an extra ten seconds for you on the day you're accidentally late.

C. Riding the Train

1 Plan for your trip. Don't wait until the day you need to be somewhere. Taking extra time to familiarize yourself with what to expect will ensure your trip is smooth and stress-free as possible.

Research the station and its location to you. You may need to take a bus or ride your bike there. Find out how long it will take you to arrive at your destination. Determine the price of your fare and if you'll need to transfer.

2 Enter the station and pay the fare. The turnstiles where you buy your ticket will be readily apparent. They accept cash, but cards are generally easier to deal with.

Look for the turnstile or gate where you can buy your fare. Never get on a train without paying the fare–getting caught is incredibly expensive and can go on your record.

3 Consider buying a pass. Passes are oftentimes cheaper than buying a ticket every day.

Do the math by multiplying each day you use the train by the cost of the ticket. Compare that number to the price of a week or month-long pass.

4 Make your way to the boarding area. If you're not sure where the boarding area is, look at a map or follow the signs.

Once you arrive at your platform, wait a safe distance from the tracks. Pay attention to where you are walking and where the train will arrive. Keep your head up and stay alert.

When the train arrives, allow other passengers to disembark before you get on. Don't stand in front of the door and expect them to walk around you; stand to the side and give them a proper room to leave the train.

5 Get on board. Get all the way on; don't let any part of you (including the straps of your bag) dangle outside of the doors.

Make sure you are on the correct train by listening to the destination and route. If you're not, get off at the next stop and reevaluate.

6 Enjoy the ride! Bring a book, download music, or play games on your phone. Always be respectful of the people around you by using headphones and keeping your music or radio show to a respectable level.

Be polite and courteous to your neighbors. Offer older people or otherwise infirm people your seat.

D.   Walking Instead of Driving

1 Walking is immeasurably better than driving. It saves you money on gas, parking, and insurance. It's great for the planet and even better for you. Walking might even be quicker than driving as some people overestimate the time they spend driving.

Consider moving closer to your work. The money you save by not having a car can help with the possible increase in rent.

2 Buy comfortable walking shoes. Nothing ruins a walk like a bad blister. Think of how much money you are saving by not driving and treat yourself!

Have your gait analyzed at a running/walking shoe store to determine which shoe is best for you.They will take the time to find the best shoe and the best fit for you.

Buy a flexible shoe. The shoe must be flexible or you might get shin splints. Twist them to see how much they bend.

Buy a shoe with cushioning. You'll be grateful to have it after a few miles after work.

3 Entertain yourself. There's no reason to go the same way every day. Change up your route and what you're doing as you walk.

Take side streets when you can (never compromise your safety) to see other neighborhoods. Talk to people you see outside. Saying hello is a great way to begin to build community.

Change up your entertainment. Listening to music, books, or radio shows can make a long walk go by in a snap.

Use your walk to think about your goals and ambitions. What do you want for yourself? What do you want for your family? What's going on at work? Exercise clears your head and you'll see and feel the results in a matter of weeks.

4 Carry a small bag with essentials you might need. Planning ahead makes small problems a snap to deal with!

Put moleskin, band aids, and antiseptic salve in it.

Carry a small water bottle. Hydration is important!

Keep a couple bucks of extra cash on you in case you need some water or to make a phone call.

Keep a spare shirt at work in case of inclement weather.

Cut expenses

Look at the ways you frivolously spend money and rethink everything. For example, avoid going to Starbucks every morning. That $4 you spend on designer coffee every morning comes out to $28 per week, or $1,460 over the course of a year!

If you're trying to save money, you may be wondering how you can reduce your expenses. Try to determine how much money you have to spend, create goals for yourself, and analyze your spending to reduce your expenses to start saving money today. These changes might seem hard at first, but switching up your daily life in small ways will add up over time.

A. Creating a Budget

1 Add up your bills and expenses. It is important to determine how much money you are spending each month. Add up all of your expenses, like your mortgage or rent, car payment, insurance payment, and grocery bill.

Include every expense that you have, no matter how small it is.

2 Subtract your expenses from your income to see how much is left. Look at your income, and then subtract all expenses that you have to pay. Once you have subtracted all of those bills from your income, you are left with how much money you have leftover to spend.

3 Write down every time you spend money. It can be easy to lose track of how much money you spend on a daily basis. Keep a note in your phone or on paper and write down each time you spend money, no matter how small. You can review what you are actually spending money on and then decide what you can cut back on.

4 Create goals for your money. If you'd like to pay off a debt, set aside money, or save up for a large purchase or trip, make those a goal for your money. If you have a goal in mind, you can start tracking your spending better and meeting deadlines that you set for yourself. This will help you stop spending money unnecessarily.

Don't get discouraged if you don't meet your goals in the timeline that you set for yourself.

5 Avoid unnecessary purchases. It can be tempting to buy cigarettes or coffee every day, but those small purchases add up over time. Try to avoid spending money on things that you don't absolutely need, until you are sure that you can afford them.

Make sure that paying your bills is your number one priority with your money.

B. Managing Your Car Expenses

1 Use public transportation as often as possible. Public transportation is good for the environment and for your wallet. Look into whether or not public transportation is cheaper than driving your own vehicle. It could help you save on gas and vehicle upkeep costs.

2 Carpool to work with your coworkers. If you live near your coworkers, see if you can start a carpool schedule with them. Ask if you can switch off days driving to work, and pick your coworkers up when it's your turn to drive. This will save you gas money and vehicle upkeep expenses.

Be sure to do your part in the carpool schedule so that you are not taking advantage of your coworkers.

3 Check your tire pressure before you drive. Your car tires have an optimal PSI that they should be at in order to use gas efficiently. Use a tire pressure gauge to determine what PSI your tires are at, and check the manual of your vehicle to see what your optimal PSI is. This will save on fuel costs over time.

If your tire pressure is low, you can fill up your tires at an air pump at most gas stations.

4 Sell your vehicle if you rarely use it. If you don't use your car often, or if you have a vehicle that you don't drive, sell it to get some money in your pocket and reduce expenses like gas and upkeep.

Check the Kelly Blue Book value of your car before you sell it so you know how much it is worth.

C. Cutting Utility Costs

1 Set your thermostat to an "away" setting when you leave the house. Turn your thermostat to 65 °F (18 °C) in the winter and 80 °F (27 °C) in the summer to keep your house warm or cool while you are gone. Check the settings on your thermostat to see if you can program it to do this automatically.

You can also set your thermostat to a less extreme setting when you are sleeping.

Tip: Consider investing in ceiling fans. They dramatically reduce the cost of heating and cooling by circulating the air more efficiently.

2 Buy energy-efficient light bulbs. Replace the light bulbs in your home with bulbs that have an "Energy Star" rating. These bulbs will cost more upfront, but they use energy more efficiently and will save you money in the long run.

You can buy energy-efficient light bulbs at most home goods and hardware stores.

3 Unplug your electronics when you aren't using them. Even if your devices are off, they are still using energy if they are

plugged in. Unplug your phone, laptop, or other chargeable devices from the wall when they are not in use to save money on your electricity bill.

Unplugging your devices also gives you protection from power surges.

4 Take 5 or 10-minute showers. Taking a shower uses multiple gallons of water each time. Keep your shower time short by using fewer products and soaping up right away once you step in the shower. Keep your water temperature lukewarm to encourage you to get out quicker, as well. This will save you money on your water bill over time.

Set a timer on your phone to remind you when your time is up.

5 Cancel your cable if you don't watch it. With the prevalence of streaming services, many people don't watch TV as often as they used to. If you have noticed that you don't watch cable anymore, cancel your subscription to save money on your monthly expenses.

When you call to cancel your cable, your provider might try to get you to keep your subscription so that they still get your money. Be polite but firm with them.

Cancel any subscription services that you aren't using, as well. These will often take out automatic monthly payments from your account that you might not even notice.

D.   Spending Less on Food and Drinks

1 Make a shopping list before you go to the store and stick to it. A shopping list gives you a clear idea of what you need and eliminates unnecessary purchases. Take a look around your kitchen to determine what you need before you go to the store, and try to stick to your list as you shop.

Tip: Try not to go grocery shopping when you are hungry. You are more likely to buy unnecessary items if you haven't eaten recently.

2 Buy fresh foods that are in season. They will cost less than the fresh food flown in from the other side of the world since the customer has to pay for the fuel that got the food there. Research the area that you live in to see what produce is in season. Local produce will often have a sign telling you where it has been grown.

Check-in your area for a local farmer's market, or buy fresh produce from your grocery store.

3 Cook meals at home as often as possible. Restaurant food is much more expensive than making a meal at home. Go out to eat as little as possible, and try to make most of your meals at home.

Try cooking meals ahead of time and then putting them in the fridge to reheat later. This will save you time and make it more likely that you won't go out to eat.

Make your lunches at home and take them to work with you so that you are less tempted to spend money on fast food.

4 Make your coffee at home instead of buying it. Buying coffee can cost you as much as $7 a day. Invest in a coffee pot and a thermos to make your own coffee and bring it with you to save money.

If you like flavored coffee, you can buy syrups and flavored creamers to make your coffee taste good.

Track down your expenses

To soar your efficiency on cutting your expenses, it is vital to keep track of them. Pick one of the numerous expense tracking applications there are around, like Money Lover or Mint, and record every single penny that goes in and out of your wallet. After 3 months or so, you should be able to know where most of your money goes and what you can do for that.

One of the issues I've always had with budgeting is that most budget reviews happen in hindsight after it's too late to do anything about it. The challenge is finding a way to measure how you're tracking against your budget without making it your new hobby. Here are six ways that I know of. (Hopefully, there's at least one that you haven't thought of before.)

1 Track by store. I love to tell the story of my friend Jenny who texted me many years ago with a budgeting quandary. Her text went something like this:

"My husband and I have budgeted how much we want to spend on different categories like clothes, food, diapers, wine, etc. That's easy to track when I buy clothes at a clothing store, food at the grocery store, wine at the liquor store, etc. But what about when I go to Target and buy all of those things? I don't have time to break all that out!"

My answer: you need a Target budget. The purpose of a budget isn't to dictate to the dollar exactly how much you'll spend on each category (although I do have a friend, Doug, who does this right down to having a budget for birdseed and cat litter). It's to give you guidelines to follow so that you can achieve your other savings goals without overdrawing your account. Rather than tracking categories, consider setting limits on what you'll spend at each store you frequent.

2 Use a separate spending account. This is what I call the "lazy person's" budget and is part of the way we do it. We have one checking account where all our bills are paid, including non-monthly things like condo association fees, life insurance and estimated taxes. We each contribute a set amount to this account each pay period, with the balance of our income going into separate checking accounts that we use for spending money. This way, we know that all the essentials will always be taken care of and the money in the separate account is "fun money," where we just dial it back on spending when the balance gets low.

3 Track as you go. This is the way I used to do it when it was just me making spending decisions. I kept a spreadsheet checking register that plotted out all my known bills ahead of time, while also keeping a running tally of my credit card balance to ensure that I didn't charge more than I could pay off each month. I still maintain this method to a certain extent to make sure that all our bills are accounted for and paid, although I no longer have to enter each and every charge into the "credit card balance due" cell.

4 Use an app. The most popular app I hear mentioned is Mint.com, which is free and connects to most of your accounts, allowing you to customize your budget and receive weekly alerts of your status. It's a bit wonky at times (it labeled my nail salon as a liquor store, although I suppose they both fall in the same category of "do you really need to spend that?") and my junk mail around personal loans and credit card offers jumped up suspiciously after signing up, but it's easy to correct transactions that are incorrectly categorized and there are other dozens of options out there besides Mint. In fact, there are entire Facebook communities dedicated to picking apart the benefits and drawbacks of each, so I won't get into those details, but if you want real-time updates on where your money is going, then an app may be your best method of tracking.

5 Try the envelope method. I first heard about the envelope method back in 2004 when a friend of mine told me she kept a "car expenses" envelope in her kitchen cupboard, where she and her husband each tucked a one hundred dollar bill each month toward future car issues and eventually a new car purchase when they needed one. When another friend mentioned her embarrassment at how much she spent on cabs each month after adding it up, I suggested she try this and it worked! Since the majority of her rides were due to poor time management that didn't allow for public transportation use, I had her put the amount she thought was reasonable to splurge on cabs in an envelope and when the envelope was empty, she had to take the bus or the train. Likewise, my colleague Greg's family uses this method to keep grocery spending in check for their family of six.

6 Download after the fact. If your concern isn't so much making sure you're not over-spending in the moment and more about just ensuring you're not mindlessly indulging in certain areas, then try my husband's method. This method is especially useful if you're just getting started and have no idea where all your money is going.

Every month he downloads his transactions into a spreadsheet (most online banking and credit card sites allow you to do this), then sorts by merchant and starts adding a label to each one – date night, concerts, gas, fast food lunches, dry cleaning, etc. When we hold our monthly money dates, he gives an update if he thinks we're going bananas in certain areas. My surprise category is always Starbucks.

There really is no right or wrong way to track your spending so try different ways until you find one that works for you and that you can stick with. It's not about the tracking. It's about making sure that you're able to achieve your other goals while still living your life.

Spend your tax refund wisely

In 2007, the average American tax refund was $2,733. That's a lot of money! Can you use that money to pay off debts or create an emergency fund instead of blowing it on something that will lose half its value the second you buy it? If you invest nearly $3,000 wisely, it could be worth ten times that much in as many years.

If you're expecting a nice tax refund this year, you may be wondering how you should spend it. It may be tempting to go on a shopping spree, but there are lots of ways you can put that money to excellent use. No matter how much money you have and what your financial goals are, you can use your tax refund to help improve your future.

A. Saving for the Future

1 Save for emergencies. Even if you don't feel like stashing your money away for the distant future, you may want to consider starting an emergency fund to help pay for unexpected expenses that can pop up at any time. Try to put a little aside so you won't have to panic if you need an x-ray or your car breaks down.

Ideally, you should have enough money in your emergency savings account to cover six months worth of expenses. In addition to helping you with unexpected expenses, this account can be a lifesaver if you end up losing your job and need cash to pay your everyday living expenses.

2 Invest in your retirement account. Most people are not saving enough for retirement, so if you fall into this group, consider giving your 401k a boost. The more money you contribute to your retirement savings account when you are young, the more it will grow.

If your employer matches your 401k contributions, it's especially worthwhile to make extra contributions because you're passing up free money if you don't.

If you don't have a 401k at work, consider opening up a Roth IRA or traditional IRA.

3 Diversify your investments. If you are already saving for retirement and emergencies, consider opening a brokerage account to invest your extra money. If you invest well, your small tax refund could turn into a big nest egg.

Depending on your preferences, you could choose to work with a broker or open your account with an online brokerage firm that allows you to do trading yourself.

While you should make smart investments, you could use this money to buy stocks that are slightly riskier than you would choose for your retirement account. They could end up paying off big!

B. Making Smart Investments

1 Invest in home improvement. Investing in your home is a great idea because you will get to enjoy the improvements while you live there, and you can feel confident that your investment will pay off when you eventually sell your home. If possible, invest in improvements that are likely to appeal to a wide array of buyers for years to come.

Energy efficient appliances, windows, and insulation will all help you save money in the long run, so they will be worth the investment.

If you can't afford the home improvement project that you really want (or need) consider stashing your tax refund in a separate account and adding more to it each month until you can afford it.

2 Invest in a business. Whether you've always dreamed of opening your own business or you already have a business that could use a little extra boost, investing your tax refund in it is a wonderful way to help make your dreams come true and offer your family more economic stability.

If you haven't started a business yet, consider starting it on the side while you continue working at your regular job. If possible, keep costs low at first.

If you already have a business, try to think of a way that you could attract new customers. You might want to invest in a marketing campaign or a store renovation, for example.

3 Go back to school or take classes. Few things are as stimulating and practical as your education. Just because you've been out of school for years doesn't mean you have to disregard the itch to learn. There are plenty of options for people who want to keep learning while working.

Get a certification in an area that is relevant to your job. It may help you earn that promotion you've been wanting.

Take night classes at your local community college or university. Whether you're working towards a degree or not, you will gain valuable knowledge.

Learn a language. Whether you choose to use computer software or a tutor who speaks natively, learning a language is a great way to keep your mind sharp while learning a bit more about a different culture.

4 Take a second look at your mortgage. If you have a mortgage on your home, you may want to consider using your tax refund to refinance it or to make an extra payment on it. Both of these options can significantly reduce the interest that you pay on your mortgage over time.

Check whether your mortgage has any prepayment penalties associated with it. Prepay fees typically range from $200 to $500, but borrowers can generally pay up to 20% of their loan balance each year before the prepay fee kicks in.

If you have a large balance on your mortgage, only make additional payments if you have already paid off your other debt and have sufficient savings.

If you do decide to prepay, make sure you stress to your lender that you want your payment to go towards your principal. If you do not specify this, the lender may not apply the amount paid towards your principal.

If you're thinking about refinancing, check current rates to make sure they are significantly lower than your current rate. Remember that you will have to pay closing costs to refinance, but you may be able to reduce your monthly payments considerably.

5 Make a tax-deductible donation. If you don't need the extra money for yourself, considering donating it to help someone who does. The advantages of donating to charity are threefold: you can make the world a better place, you can make yourself happy by doing something good, and you can write off the charitable donation on next year's taxes.

Be sure to hold on to the receipt from the charity so you will have evidence of your donation when it's time to do your taxes next year.

C. Improving Your Family's Well-Being

1 Pay off your debt. Whether you have credit card debt, a car loan, or student loans, consider using your tax refund to pay them off (or at least make a dent in them). Not only will you feel much better without all this debt, but you will also have extra income each month once it's paid off.

If you have several sources of debt, pay off the debt with the highest interest rate first. This is the loan that you are paying the most interest on, so it makes sense to eliminate it first. Then pay off the debt with the second-highest interest rate, and so on, until all your debt is paid off. This is known as the avalanche method.

Another method, known as snowballing, takes the opposite approach. You pay off the smallest debt, thereby immediately eliminating one payment from your list of debts (paying of your largest debt or the debt with the highest interest payment may take some time while paying off your smallest debt can potentially be done in a single payment). This has the added benefit of improving your morale and motivation — these "quick wins" will make paying off all your debt seem more doable.

2 Invest in your children's education. If you have children, the thought of having to pay for college one day is probably

terrifying. That's why it's a good idea to start college savings accounts for them when they're young. If you contribute a small amount each year, it can really add up.

If you contribute to a 529 account, you may be able to deduct the contribution from your state income taxes (depending on where you live). With this kind of account, you can withdraw the money tax-free as long as it is used for educational purposes.

3 Take care of the essentials. If you've been putting off buying something that you genuinely need because you couldn't afford it, there may be no better use for this money. Depending on your needs, this may mean getting your car repaired, replacing your broken washing machine, or getting your kids some new clothes.

Keep in mind that putting off necessary expenses can often end up costing you more in the long run. Take care of them as soon as possible to avoid ending up in an emergency situation.

4 Get insured. Insurance can be expensive, but it provides essential security if something bad happens in the future. If your family isn't sufficiently insured, consider using your tax refund to invest in some much-needed peace of mind.

If you don't already have health insurance, you should seriously consider investing in a policy. If you do not have one available to you through work, you can purchase an individual or family policy through the federal health insurance marketplace or through your state's marketplace.

Get life insurance if you have a spouse or children who depend on your salary.You can get two types of life insurance: whole life and term insurance. Rates vary depending on your age, health, and other factors, but you may be able to get a good amount of coverage for just a few hundred dollars a year.

You may also want to consider increasing your homeowner's insurance to protect you from potential damages or purchasing an umbrella policy to protect you from liability if someone is injured on your property.

5 Invest in a Health Savings Account (HSA). Health insurance doesn't cover all medical expenses. An HSA is a savings account that you can use to set aside tax-free money for a wide variety of medical expenses, including deductibles and copayments. Many employers offer these accounts, and you may be able to open one at a bank if your employer doesn't.

There is a cap on how much you can deposit into an HSA each year, but you can choose to keep contributing money and saving it for medical expenses that occur later in life rather than paying for every current medical expense with it.

Break up with your credit card.

Did you know that people who use credit cards for purchases end up spending more money than people who use cash? That's because parting with cash is painful. Using a credit card doesn't carry that much of a sting. If you can, divorce your credit card and see how it feels to pay with cash. You'll probably end up saving a boatload of money.

If you do maintain a credit card, do things to reduce expenses. Try to pay off the full balance each month and on time. That results in interest-free credit. At the very least, make the monthly minimum payment before the due date to avoid a late fee.

While a widely used credit card can be an asset, a poorly managed one can be toxic. Divorcing yourself from your credit card for all but the most essential purchases is one way to rein in bad spending habits, and learning to pay cash again for most things will bring back a sense of value into your shopping choices. But like any breakup, the process may be painful and there may be moments of temptation to return to spend-as-you-like. Finding a simple route to ridding yourself of credit debt will help you to live more freely, within your means.

A. Assessing your current credit use

1 Scrutinize your credit card bill to determine what you're spending money on each month. Sometimes you may not even realize how much you're charging until you see it in black and white. Plus, because credit card fraud has become commonplace you may be paying for items you haven't even purchased. (You have been checking monthly, haven't you? If not, goodness knows whose boots, restaurant meals and movie tickets you've been funding!)

Look for a consistent pattern each month. Compare and contrast three months worth of credit card bills to look for trends. For example, are you purchasing a $5.50 latte and $3.00 scone every morning? How often do you shop or dine out and then use your credit card?

Add up your monthly credit card expenses, along with other financial obligations such as mortgage payments, utilities and groceries. Identify every bill that must be paid each month in addition to your credit card bill. Don't forget about childcare, school tuition and gas (if you don't pay for gas using your credit card).

Compare your monthly expenses to your total household income. Are you spending more money than you bring home each month and if so, where is the bulk of it going? Typically, the largest amount should go toward the mortgage or rent, so concentrate what is being spent on luxury items such as clothing, entertainment, and dining out.

Find luxury items you can do without. Tally up the consistent expense and reduce it from the total. Compare your new total to your household income and determine if you are living within your means. If you still are not, go back through your list and cut other expenses. While most people consider cable television to be in the "need" instead of "want" pile, you should consider transferring it to the "want" pile until you can get your credit cards under control.

2 Identify how much money you are sending to your credit card company each month. If it's the minimum balance, there's a good chance you'll end up paying double for your purchases in the long run. Credit card interest rates can exceed 30%, so figure out how much of your money your credit card company is making off of you for only paying that small portion each month.

B. Divorcing your credit card

1 Stop using the credit card. Now that you've identified what you've been using credit for, and what it's costing you, focus on two things—the first is paying off the debt, and the second is not using credit for anything that cannot be paid back within the no-interest period. For many people, it is easiest to go cold turkey and stop using the card until it has been paid off, then reassessing its usage after the change. Remove credit cards from your wallet—except for your debit card. This maneuver may be a little painful at first, especially if your first inclination is to reach for your credit card; however, it's likely to be your best line of defense. Some ideas for putting the use of credit temporarily beyond your reach include:

Keep your credit cards in a safe location at home. Don't just throw them in a junk drawer or in an area where someone can pick them up and use them. Consider placing them in a file or even a home safe.

Place the card into a plastic container, fill water, and place it in the freezer. You have to think long and hard before using it now!

Resolve to reduce multiple cards to one. You could cut up all the other cards and put the chosen one somewhere safe for now. Some people don't recommend taking the scissors to all of your credit cards though, as you may need them in the future. For any cards you do decide you no longer want, be sure to go through the steps of actively closing your account, or your credit card provider may eventually apply inactivity fees to your account.

Remind yourself constantly that anything placed on a credit card tends to cost you twice as much, thanks to fees for payments outside the interest-free period.

2 If you prefer to pay with plastic, use your debit card. Understand the consequences though—if your checking account is empty, you may be rejected at the register. If you're concerned about being rejected, talk to your banker about arranging for overdraft protection (which may mean a fee) or linking your checking, savings and a line of credit to be used as a backup. However, a few times of embarrassment can pay dividends in a lifetime of keeping an active memory of just how much money you really have to spend...

Use Internet banking to keep tabs on your expenses. In order to know what you have in your account, log onto your bank's Internet banking system at least once daily to keep tabs on what you have (and don't have). Also, consider using direct deposit for your checks to reduce the amount of time it takes for your paycheck to clear.

Some companies will only accept credit cards, such as airlines and stadium venues. In this case, you may need to keep a credit card handy but keep to the rule that you should be able to cover the cost either immediately or within the non-interest payment period. Another alternative is to give the exact cash to a friend or family member who can pay using their credit card on your behalf.

Consider switching to prepaid credit cards with a limit for online purchases. This protects you from fraud (the card limit is all that there is to use) and it will stop you from overspending on online shopping.

C. Restoring the cash culture

1 Cut out all extra (non-essential) spending that cannot be covered with cash. If your debit card or cash cannot cover the expense, don't buy it. This may mean going without buying new items for several months (anything from outfits to electronics). However, if you truly want to live within your means and free yourself from credit card debt, you'll need to adhere to spending within—or preferably below—your means. Other money-saving ideas include:

Brew coffee at home and/or brown bag it for lunch. If your morning latte as part of your routine, you can most likely save a significant amount of money just by having your coffee at home or bringing your lunch to work. If you don't believe this, place the same amount of money it costs for that daily treat into a jar each day. Add it up at the end of the week. Multiply it by 52 weeks a year. And you will be convinced that this money soon adds up!

Carpool with friends to work or school. With gas prices on the rise, carpooling is more popular than ever. Carpoolers can slash their gas budget and wear and tear on their vehicle, which saves at the pump and the auto shop.

Go vintage. Hit the secondhand and thrift stores and make what was once old into something new again. The great revival of craft, DIY, and restoration is making it not only acceptable but desirable to be fixing things up from the past to make them work for your future. There are plenty of great library books and free online articles on recycling old stuff into new goodies, so you don't even need to fork out any money to find out how!

Find homemade food alternatives for food you used to purchase when out. Perhaps there's an undiscovered baker, fast food chef or soul food cook within you that's waiting to burst forth. Now's your chance to find out.

2 Create a new budget that revolves solely around using cash. This may mean cutting out Friday night dinners at your favorite restaurant but in the long run, you will be in better financial shape (you might even get a little healthier if your favorite weekly splurge was a calorie-laden feast!). Living on cash means you need to reorient your expectations about payments for things, placing the essentials at the top and non-

essentials last in the queue. It may feel deprived at first, but this feeling changes when you start to savor the things you can afford and realize that instant buying ability tends to lead to poor choices and clutter. In a short space of time, you will discover a great sense of liberty in being able to cover your expenses and treats with cash and not have to pay for them later.

Time your bills with the arrival of your paycheck. If you are living paycheck to paycheck (now that you cannot charge many items), make sure you can cover all your primary bills first by writing down the dates they are due as compared to when you get paid.

Apply surplus cash after your bills are paid to cover credit card expenses. Consider food, gas, and other necessary living expenses before paying your credit card bills. Also, if possible start saving through either an IRA or a high-interest CD.

3 Pay down your balance each month. This means sending more than the minimum required amount to your credit card company. The best way to get out from underneath credit card debt is to pay as much as you can each month.

Set aside a specific amount each month to send to your credit card company(s). Consider how long it'll take you to pay off each card, taking interest into consideration.

Look for balance transfer offers to lower your interest rate. One way you can reduce your overall total is to take advantage of balance transfer promotions through your financial institution. However, inquire about transfer fees and teaser rates to ensure you will receive the same low rate for the life of the loan.

Ask your credit card company for a lower interest rate. It never hurts to ask, plus you should also ask that the annual fee be waived. Tell the credit card company that you plan to transfer your (massive) balance to another card and then see what they can do for you.

4 Spend time reflecting on the value of money, your effort and your time. Spending cash most of the time returns a keen sense of just how many hours of your labor it takes to earn an item and you soon become less willing to part with cash for poor quality or over-hyped fads. Thinking about how money is used and valued in your own life will let you face the financial truths rather than wish them away. There are plenty of excellent books and articles on good financial management—find one that has a style you like and start practicing some of its ideas to stay credit card debt-free.

Be aware that speed is what our societies worship. Wanting things now and getting things done now is marketed as a sign of being hip, while it's implied that going slowly is uncool. Yet, it's never uncool to think carefully, decrease your debt and resist unnecessary purchases. Slow down, earn what you buy and really appreciate it.

CHAPTER NO 5: GOING MORTGAGE FREE

Refinance your home mortgage.

Refinance to a lower rate or to a 15-year loan instead of a 30-year loan. This way you only pay a few extra hundred dollars per month but you will save yourself much more than that in total interest.

For example, a $200,000 mortgage on a 30-year loan will cost you another $186,500 in interest payments, so you are actually paying a total of $386,500 over the course of 30 years. On the other hand, if you are willing to pay a few extra hundred dollars a month (for example, $350) by refinancing to a 15-year loan (usually at a lower interest rate), you could pay your mortgage off in only 15 years, and the best part is you would save yourself a whopping $123,700 in interest. That's money in your pocket. Talk to a loan officer about your options.

Refinancing a mortgage means paying off an existing loan and replacing it with a new one. There are many reasons why homeowners refinance: to obtain a lower interest rate; to shorten the term of their mortgage; to convert from an adjustable-rate mortgage (ARM) to a fixed-rate mortgage, or vice versa; to tap into home equity to raise funds to deal with a financial emergency, finance a large purchase, or consolidate debt.

Since refinancing can cost between 2% and 5% of a loan's principal and—as with an original mortgage—requires an appraisal, title search, and application fees, it's important for a homeowner to determine whether refinancing is a wise financial decision.

A. Refinancing to Secure a Lower Interest Rate

One of the best reasons to refinance is to lower the interest rate on your existing loan. Historically, the rule of thumb is that refinancing is a good idea if you can reduce your interest rate by at least 2%. However, many lenders say 1% savings is enough of an incentive to refinance.

B. KEY TAKEAWAYS

Getting a mortgage with a lower interest rate is one of the best reasons to refinance.

When interest rates drop, consider refinancing to shorten the term of your mortgage and pay significantly less in interest payments.

Switching to a fixed-rate mortgage—or to an adjustable-rate one—can make sense depending on the rates and how long you plan to remain in your current home.

Tapping equity or consolidating debt can be good reasons to refinance—or doing so can sometimes make the debt trap worse.

Reducing your interest rate not only helps you save money, but it also increases the rate at which you build equity in your home, and it can decrease the size of your monthly payment. For example, a 30-year fixed-rate mortgage with an interest rate of 5.5% on a $100,000 home has a principal and interest payment of $568. That same loan at 4.1% reduces your payment to $483.

C. Refinancing to Shorten the Loan's Term

When interest rates fall, homeowners sometimes have the opportunity to refinance an existing loan for another loan that, without much change in the monthly payment, has a significantly shorter term. For a 30-year fixed-rate mortgage on a $100,000 home, refinancing from 9% to 5.5% can cut the term in half to 15 years with only a slight change in the monthly payment from $804.62 to $817.08. However, if you're already at 5.5% for 30 years ($568), getting a 3.5% mortgage for 15 years would raise your payment to $715. So do the math and see what works.

D. Refinancing to Convert to an Adjustable-Rate or Fixed-Rate Mortgage

While ARMs often start out offering lower rates than fixed-rate mortgages, periodic adjustments can result in rate increases that are higher than the rate available through a fixed-rate mortgage.[2] When this occurs, converting to a fixed-rate mortgage results in a lower interest rate and eliminates concern over future interest rate hikes.

Conversely, converting from a fixed-rate loan to an ARM—which often has a lower monthly payment than a fixed-term mortgage—can be a sound financial strategy if interest rates are falling, especially for homeowners who do not play to stay in their homes for more than a few years. These homeowners can reduce their loan's interest rate and monthly payment, but they will not have to worry about how higher rates go 30 years in the future.

If rates continue to fall, the periodic rate adjustments on an ARM result in decreasing rates and smaller monthly mortgage payments eliminating the need to refinance every time rates drop. With mortgage interest rates rising, on the other hand, this would be an unwise strategy.

E. Refinancing to Tap Equity or Consolidate Debt

While the previously mentioned reasons to refinance are all financially sound, mortgage refinancing can be a slippery slope to never-ending debt.

Homeowners often access the equity in their homes to cover major expenses, such as the costs of home remodeling or a child's college education. These homeowners may justify the refinancing by the fact that remodeling adds value to the home or that the interest rate on the mortgage loan is less than the rate on money borrowed from another source.

Another justification is that the interest on mortgages is tax deductible. While these arguments may be true, increasing the number of years that you owe on your mortgage is rarely a smart financial decision nor is spending a dollar on interest to get a 30-cent tax deduction. Also note that since the Tax Cut and Jobs Act went into effect, the size of the loan on which you can deduct interest has dropped from $1 million to $750,000 if you bought your house after Dec. 15, 2017.[4]

Many homeowners refinance to consolidate their debt. At face value, replacing high-interest debt with a low-interest mortgage is a good idea. Unfortunately, refinancing does not bring automatic financial prudence. Take this step only if you are convinced you can resist the temptation to spend once the refinancing relieves you from debt.

It takes years to recoup the 3% to 6% of principal that refinancing costs, so don't do it unless you plan to stay in your current home for more than a few years.

Be aware that a large percentage of people who once generated high-interest debt on credit cards, cars, and other purchases will simply do it again after the mortgage refinancing gives them the available credit to do so. This creates an instant quadruple loss composed of wasted fees on the refinancing, lost equity in the house, additional years of increased interest payments on the new mortgage, and the return of high-interest debt once the credit cards are maxed out again—the possible result is an endless perpetuation of the debt cycle and eventual bankruptcy.

Another reason to refinance can be a serious financial emergency. If that is the case, carefully research all your options for raising funds before you take this step. If you do a cash-out refinance, you may be charged a higher interest rate on the new mortgage than for a rate-and-term refinance, in which you don't take out money.

F. The Bottom Line

Refinancing can be a great financial move if it reduces your mortgage payment, shortens the term of your loan, or helps you build equity more quickly. When used carefully, it can also be a valuable tool for bringing debt under control. Before you refinance, take a careful look at your financial situation and ask yourself: How long do I plan to continue living in the house? How much money will I save by refinancing?

The Tax Cut and Jobs Act has changed the size of the loan from which you can deduct interest: it has dropped from $1 million to $750,000 if you bought your house after Dec. 15, 2017.

Again, keep in mind that refinancing costs 2% to 5% of the loan's principal. It takes years to recoup that cost with the savings generated by a lower interest rate or a shorter term. So, if you are not planning to stay in the home for more than a few years, the cost of refinancing may negate any of the potential savings. It also pays to remember that a savvy homeowner is always looking for ways to reduce debt, build equity, save money, and eliminate their mortgage payment. Taking cash out of your equity when you refinance does not help to achieve any of those goals.

www.ingramcontent.com/pod-product-compliance
Lightning Source LLC
Chambersburg PA
CBHW030637220526
45463CB00004B/1549